PRAISE FOR

"To say that Noah St. John changed our lives is the understatement of the century. Before hiring Noah as my personal coach, I had a brochure website that wasn't bringing in any money. Today, I have my own online store that makes me money in my sleep. Thank you, Noah, for bringing out the greatness in me that I didn't even know I had!"

—Dr. Stacey Cooper, chiropractor

"Before I heard Noah speak, I had been a failure at everything I touched. After using his methods, I built the largest infill development company in Nashville with over $40 million in sales. Thank you, Noah; keep doing what you're doing because a lot of people need you!"

—Britnie Turner Keane,
CEO of Aerial Development Group

"I highly recommend Dr. Noah St. John as a keynote speaker because he's not only different from other speakers, he also truly cares about his clients and resonates on a deep emotional level with his audience. He's dynamic, impactful, inspiring, motivating, and professional—in short, the PERFECT speaker!"

—Lauren Ashley Kay, meeting planner

"Dr. Noah St. John has been a Legend in the industry of speaking and motivating for many years. His reputation as a home-run speaker, powerful coach, and performance expert is among the best in the world. More importantly, his home life, family, and ability to balance both business and the living of a wonderful life are inspiring to his peers and clients. He is an example to all who know him."

—Jason Hewlett, CSP, CPAE,
author of *The Promise to the One*

"Noah's methods helped me get through a particularly challenging time in my life. If you're thinking about hiring Noah as a coach, trainer, or speaker, don't think about it another minute—just DO it, because his strategies have the power to change lives!"

—Mari Smith, premier Facebook marketing
expert and social media thought Leader

"Noah's methods can transform your life and help you create the masterpiece you truly want and are capable of achieving."   —John Assaraf, featured in *The Secret*

"Noah's training was instrumental in helping me bounce back and into major profits. His insights on removing head trash are unlike anything I've ever seen!"

—Ray Higdon, author of *Time, Money, Freedom*

"Noah St. John helped me gain the mental edge I was looking for. His methods helped me perform at my highest level without strain, and I saw better results immediately using his system."

—Andre Branch, NFL football player

"Before being coached by Noah, I was holding myself back out of fear. Since working with Noah, I've built a multi-million dollar company in less than two years. I highly recommend coaching with Noah, because I guarantee it will change your life, like it changed mine!"

—Tim Taylor, real estate professional

"Noah St. John has been at the forefront of the business coaching industry for more than two decades now. He's the best in the business when it comes to helping entrepreneurs skyrocket their results in record time. If you want to take your business to a whole new level without the stress or overwhelm, hire Noah St. John TODAY. You'll be glad you did!"

—Anik Singal, Lurn.com, 8-figure CEO

ALSO BY NOAH ST. JOHN, PhD

*The 7-Figure Expert: Your Ultimate Guide to a Life
of More Impact, Influence, and Financial Freedom*

*The 7-Figure Chiropractor:
Your Ultimate Guide to Scale Up Your
Practice and Live a Freedom Lifestyle*

*The 7-Figure Life: How to Leverage The 4 Focus
Factors for More Wealth and Happiness*

*Power Habits®: The New Science
for Making Success Automatic®*

*AFFORMATIONS®:
The Miracle of Positive Self-Talk*

*Millionaire AFFORMATIONS®:
The Magic Formula That Will Make You Rich*

*Millionaire AFFORMATIONS® Journal:
The Magic Habit Formula That Will Make You Rich*

Take Out Your Head Trash about Money

The Secret Code of Success

Permission to Succeed®

Available at NoahStJohn.com
or wherever books are sold

THE
POWER
HABITS®
OF UNSTOPPABLE
SELF-CONFIDENCE

UNCOVER THE SECRET
TO UNLOCK YOUR
FULL POTENTIAL

Dr. Noah St. John

Published 2023 by Gildan Media LLC
aka G&D Media
www.GandDmedia.com

FIRST EDITION: 2023

Front cover design by David Rheinhardt of Pyrographx

Library of Congress Cataloging-in-Publication Data is available upon request

ISBN: 978-1-7225-0651-3

10   9   8   7   6   5   4   3   2   1

This book is dedicated to #Afformers and
#AfformationWarriors around the world:
Those brave souls who ask better questions
to make this a better world
for all of God's creatures.
And to my beautiful wife, Babette,
for being the best example of a Loving Mirror
I've ever met.

Contents

Introduction

How Your Life Can Change In Just 12 Weeks

Believe you can and you're halfway there.
—THEODORE ROOSEVELT

In November 2020, the world was in the depths of the global pandemic. For months, it seemed as though everything was shut down and our future was uncertain. It was all fear, fear, fear.

That year, on the Saturday before Thanksgiving, I woke up at five in the morning with a vision. It came completely out of the blue, and it said, "We're supposed to move."

Have you ever had one of those inner knowings that told you something that didn't make any logical sense—yet you listened to it, because you knew it came from your higher knowing or intuitive self? You've had that happen to you too, right?

When this happened to me, I thought, "What do you mean, we're supposed to move?" My wife, Babette, and I were living in a pleasant upper-middle-class house in a nice neighborhood, so moving to a new one was the furthest thing from my mind.

Yet I couldn't shake that inner knowing, that vision, that woke me up early that morning. So I thought, "Maybe we can move in, say, six months to a year. After all, there's no hurry, right?"

So I got out of bed, turned on my computer, and started looking on real estate websites for homes in my area. Click, click, click—with no sense of urgency or even knowing what I was looking for.

Suddenly, I came upon a house—no, a mansion—no, a mansion on a hill—no, a mansion on a hill in a beautiful location—and I thought:

"*What?*

"This house is *stunning.*

"This house is *incredible.*

"This house is a *mansion on a hill.*

"It's *in my price range.*

"It's *10 minutes from where I'm sitting right now.*

"And *the price just dropped.*"

And *there was going to be an open house the next day*—yes, the Sunday before Thanksgiving 2020.

So I wake up Babette and say, "Honey, wanna go look at a house tomorrow?"

She says, "Sure!"

The next day, as we pull up the driveway to this magnificent mansion, she takes one look at the house and says, "I'm packing tonight."

Eighty-three days later, we moved into that magnificent mansion on a hill.

Yes, that's just one day less than 12 weeks—we even celebrated our tenth wedding anniversary in our new mansion on a hill!

So yes, your life CAN change in less than 12 weeks—if you're willing to take the ACTION to make it happen!

What does this story mean for you?

Whether this is the first personal growth book you've ever read or the hundredth, one thing I know about you (because you're reading this right now) is that you're passionate about wanting to improve your life.

I'm Just Like You

Like you, I'm passionate about self-improvement. You see, I grew up poor in a rich neighborhood. I know that's a total cliché, but it's totally true. I grew up in a little town called Kennebunkport, Maine—which happens to be one of the wealthiest communities in New England.

However, my family was dirt-poor. I mean that literally, because we lived at the bottom of a dirt road in a drafty, unfinished house that my parents ended up losing to foreclosure when I was just fifteen years old.

What I remember most about my childhood is my parents arguing all the time. What did they argue about? You're right—money . . . and the fact that we didn't have any.

Like millions of other parents, my parents worked hard and sacrificed to put food on the table and keep our family fed. But no matter how hard they tried, my parents could never seem to get ahead.

That's why, growing up, I saw first-hand the enormous chasm between the haves—which was everyone else in the community—and the have-nots, who were my family.

That's also why, from a very young age, I was determined that I was not going to live a life of poverty, fear, lack and not-enoughness—even though that was the only life I had ever known.

The problem was that I didn't have anyone I could turn to who could help me, coach me, or teach me how to be successful. So I turned to the only resource I had—the town library. Growing up, I would spend all of my days after school in the library, reading books on personal and spiritual growth—the classics by authors like Dale Carnegie, Napoleon Hill, Stephen Covey, Wayne Dyer, and more.

> GROWING UP, I EXPERIENCED FIRSTHAND THE GAP BETWEEN THE HAVES AND HAVE-NOTS.

Many years later, when I was a religious studies major in college, I would drive around in my 1986 Subaru station wagon listening to self-improvement audiotapes (yes, this was when audiotapes were still a thing!).

My Dream to Make a Difference

Year after year, I would daydream and think, "Wouldn't it be amazing if *I* could be a best-selling author, keynote speaker and in-demand coach? Wouldn't it be incredible if people were driving around in *their* cars listening to *my* audio programs?"

In 1997, I had two epiphanies that changed the course of my life: I discovered the essential missing piece in the field of mental health and personal development. That led me to write and self-publish my first book, *Permission to Succeed®*. In 1999, it was published by the publisher of the Chicken Soup for the Soul series in 1999.

Then I published another book, and another, and yet another . . .

After I'd been in business for over ten years, I had written nine books, authored hundreds of articles, and was coaching seven-and eight-figure CEOs and consulting with leading companies and organizations on personal growth and business development. And I kept seeing the difference that my work was making in the lives of my coaching clients:

WHEN MY CLIENTS FOLLOW MY SYSTEM, THEY GET LIFE-CHANGING RESULTS.

- Mike doubled his income twice in 12 weeks.
- Susan went from $60,000 in debt to a six-figure income in less than 12 weeks.
- Camille lost 200 pounds and kept it off, after trying every diet and exercise program on the planet.
- Steven's business increased by 800 percent in less than 12 weeks.
- Adam's company went from being stuck at $4 million in revenues to over $20 million in less than 18 months.
- . . . and hundreds more.

I saw that when my clients followed my formula, they kept getting amazing results.

That's how, years after I was driving around in my old Subaru station wagon, dreaming of the day I would be a best-selling author, keynote speaker, and in-demand mental health coach, my dream finally came true.

Welcome to Your New Life

I'm thrilled to welcome you to this life-changing journey into the Power Habits® of Unstoppable Self-Confidence. The true story I just shared with you is just one example of what can happen when you start to apply the Power Habits of Unstoppable Self-Confidence that I'll be sharing with you in this book.

For years, I *wished* that "someday" my dream would come true. I fervently *hoped* it would happen. Yet *wishing* and *hoping* do NOT make things happen!

In fact, it wasn't until I worked deeply on myself, using the strategies I'll share with you in this book, that I finally developed the self-confidence to TAKE ACTION in the face of my fears!

What does this mean for you? When you apply the methods I'll teach you in this book, you too can develop the kind of unstoppable self-confidence to take action in YOUR life—and even do things you didn't think you could do!

I'll also be sharing real-life stories of some of my coaching clients who followed my formula and saw incredible transformations in their lives, careers, and businesses.

Welcome to your new life!

Remember: I believe in you.

Your Coach,
Noah St. John, PhD

1

Unlocking Your Unstoppable Self-Confidence

Once we believe in ourselves, we can risk curiosity, wonder, spontaneous delight, or any experience that reveals the human spirit.

—E E CUMMINGS

As we begin this journey together, let me give you the big picture of what you can expect to get and some of the amazing benefits you can expect to see as a result of following the strategies I'll give you in this book.

First, we're going to look at self-confidence in a new way. We'll examine many of the myths surrounding this subject and why holding on to them may be hurting your self-confidence right now.

We'll also dive deeply into the four main areas where self-confidence plays a crucial role in your life: your *relationships,* your *career,* your *finances,* and your *happiness.*

The Four Main Benefits of Unstoppable Self-Confidence

First, when you apply the habits I'll teach you in this book, your ability to have happier and healthier relationships will be greatly improved. Today many people find themselves in relationships that are broken, unhappy, or unfulfilling. We also know that it can be harder than ever to create meaningful friendships with other people because so many traditional social structures that many of us grew up with are gone for good.

However, when you follow the steps in this book, your ability to meet, attract, and create lasting friendships and loving relationships will improve significantly.

Second, you will find that with increased self-confidence will come marked improvement in your career or business. I know you've seen it a thousand times before: someone with less talent, skill, and intelligence than you who seems to get everything they want—while you're still working like crazy and NOT getting ahead!

"How do they do it?" you wonder, envying their supreme self-confidence and success.

When you follow the steps in this book, you too will become one of those "lucky" few who always seem to be in the right place at the right time, doing the right thing with the right people and getting the right results.

HAVE YOU EVER WONDERED, "HOW DO THEY DO IT?"

Third, there's no question that self-confidence plays a huge role in your finances and the wealth you attain in life. Have you ever wondered what it would feel like to wake up every day, knowing that you can attract all the money you want? How would you like to have true financial freedom so you could spend more time with your family, doing the things you really want to do?

Many of my coaching clients have found that by following my methods, they've been able to create a new level of wealth and success, for example:

- Getting their first book published
- Landing their dream job
- Growing their business by six, seven, even eight figures

- Reaching their personal and financial goals twice as fast with half the effort
- Making more in just 12 weeks than they'd made in the previous 12 months, while winning their lives back

Finally, when you activate the Power Habits of Unstoppable Self-Confidence, you'll find that you'll have a new-found sense of happiness, enthusiasm, and zest for life—that wonderful feeling of fulfillment and peace of mind that comes from knowing you are *being and expressing the person you were meant to be.*

In fact, you'll discover that self-confidence and happiness go hand in hand—because without one, it's awfully hard to experience the other. That's why, as you follow my formula, you'll find that as your level of self-confidence goes up, so will your level of happiness!

The Seven Big Questions about Self-Confidence

As we begin our journey into the Power Habits of Unstoppable Self-Confidence, let me share with you some of the biggest questions my clients ask me on this subject:

1. What is self-confidence, and why is it so important?

2. What are some of the biggest myths about self-confidence?

3. Are self-confident people born that way, or is it something they've worked at?

4. Can anyone become self-confident, or is it something reserved for just a lucky few?

5. I've always been shy. What if these methods just don't work for me?

6. I'm scared of public speaking or meeting new people. Is this about doing a bunch of crazy things that will make me uncomfortable?

7. Can something as difficult to master as self-confidence really be taught, and can it be broken down into simple steps that anyone can learn?

After coaching thousands of entrepreneurs, companies, teams, and organizations in over 120 countries for the last 25 years, let me assure you that the answer to that last question is a resounding YES!

In fact, if you want to look at an example of someone who went from having *zero* self-confidence to having unstoppable self-confidence, you don't have to look any further than the author of this book.

I'M LIVING PROOF THAT ANYONE CAN LEARN THESE HABITS.

The Nerdiest Nerd in the Industry

When I was growing up, my teachers always loved me, because I always did my homework and got straight A's all the way through grade school, middle school, and high school.

Yes, I was one of those kids who always knew the answer and handed in their homework perfectly and on time. For all you Harry Potter fans, I was Hermione.

I honestly thought that was the secret of success: do your homework and do what your teachers tell you to do.

It wasn't until I got out in the real world that I realized that getting straight A's in school did not guarantee success in life. In fact, the more I studied success and interviewed hundreds of highly successful people, I realized that getting straight A's in school may have been one of the worst things I could have done.

Why? Well, think about this for a moment. How many times have you heard a highly successful person talk about the fact that they didn't do well in school or actually did very poorly in school? It happens so often, it's a cliché.

For example, author Malcolm Gladwell talks about this in his book *David and Goliath,* where he showed that a disproportionate number of highly successful CEOs have "learning disabilities" like dyslexia. The point is that someone who has a learning disorder has to learn how to get along with people and how to get people to like you.

Me? I was exactly the opposite. I loved reading books and doing homework. I craved that feeling of getting A's on my papers and would be very depressed if I ever got a B or, heaven forbid, a B minus. And of course, to get a C was completely out of the question.

When I got out into the *real world*, I was stunned by the fact that getting straight A's not only *didn't* guarantee success in life, it actually seemed to be a *hindrance!*

There's an old phrase in business: "When you get out of school, you'll find A students working for C students." That's because at school the C students were doing things like talking to their classmates, socializing, going to parties, and learning how to get along with people—all the stuff that I thought was stupid and a waste of time!

So there I was, a National Merit Scholar and straight A student, with no clue how to succeed in the real world. It also didn't help that at the age

IN THE REAL WORLD, A STUDENTS TEND TO WORK FOR C STUDENTS.

of nineteen, after my first year of college, I decided to become a professional ballet dancer.

Yes, a professional ballet dancer, like Mikhail Baryshnikov, only nowhere nearly as good. My body was *not* built for ballet, and besides I had no self-confidence whatsoever—which meant that any time the director would criticize me (which was all the time), I would beat myself up and try that much harder to get it right.

That's why it's no surprise that after just three years of physical punishment, my body gave out, and a career-ending injury forced me to retire from professional ballet at the age of twenty-two. And that's how I found myself on the street with no job, no money, no friends, no connections, and no idea how to succeed in the real world.

That's why I hope you realize that when I talk with you about how important it is to learn and master the Power Habits of Unstoppable Self-Confidence, it comes from hard-won knowledge of what it means to work your way up from the bottom of the barrel.

What Is Self-Confidence?

So now, let's look at the first question that many of my coaching clients ask me: What is self confidence, and why is it so important?

While there are many different opinions on this, to me, self-confidence is simply *the belief that you can do what you set out to do.*

It's the belief that you can and will reach your goals and accomplish what you set out to do, no matter what the obstacles.

Self-confidence is known by other names like *self-worth, self-image,* and *self-esteem.* While none of these are right or wrong, I've observed that each of these terms is talking about something slightly different.

Self-worth refers to the value that you place on yourself and your contribution to society and the world.

Self-image means how you see yourself and what you see when you look in the mirror.

Self-esteem refers to your opinion of yourself and how good or bad you feel about yourself in general.

While all of these are important, in my opinion self-confidence is the most important, because it affects every aspect of your life.

To look at self-confidence in another way, let's think about what happens if you don't have self-confidence.

What If You Don't Have Self-Confidence?

If you don't have self-confidence, you won't have the belief that you can reach your goals. That means, at the first roadblock, setback, or bump in the road, you will quit or give up on your dreams.

If you don't have self-confidence, you won't speak up for yourself at the next board meeting or sales presentation. And if you don't speak up for yourself, you'll have to settle for whatever the world gives you—and many times, the world won't give you much, unless you speak up and ask for it.

If you don't have self-confidence, you won't walk up to the person you'd like to meet at the next social gathering. You'll miss out on the chance to meet someone who could become a good friend or business colleague—or even the love of your life. If you don't have self-confidence, you won't call that person you met, which means you could miss out on a potentially life-changing relationship.

If you don't have self-confidence, you'll have to settle for whatever crumbs are left over after those who do have self-confidence have helped themselves to the bounty of life. I regret to admit that that's what I did for the first forty years of my life.

I SETTLED FOR THE CRUMBS OF LIFE FOR FORTY YEARS.

Why Do So Few People Have Self-Confidence?

If self-confidence is so vitally important to your relationships, your career, your finances, and your happiness . . .

How come so few people actually have self-confidence? Why is it that most people aren't very self-confident, but the few people who have it seem to have everything handed to them on a silver platter?

One main reason is that most of us were trained from a very young age not to be self-confident. Well-meaning parents and teachers tell us things like, "Don't talk too highly of yourself," "Don't be arrogant," and "Don't get too big for your britches." (Who wears britches, anyway? And why are they always so small?)

Most of us were taught by well-meaning parents or caregivers to be "nice" and not make noise. Naturally, this was meant for our good and for the good of society, because society wouldn't function very well if we all didn't try to get along with one another.

Unfortunately, many of us—especially those who are hypersensitive or afraid of criticism—took this advice a bit too far. Instead of taking it to mean that we should get along with others, we interpreted it to mean that shouldn't stand up or speak up for ourselves. That's certainly what happened with me.

SOME OF US TOOK BEING NICE TOO LITERALLY.

Growing up, my parents made it clear that children should be seen and not heard. (Better still, if I were *not* seen and *not* heard!) While I'm sure they had only the best intentions, I interpreted their spoken and unspoken messages to mean that I should just shut up and be happy with whatever life handed to me, even if it wasn't what I wanted. It wasn't until many years later—and only after spending a small fortune on every personal growth program on the planet—that I finally learned that if I wanted something from life, I had to open my mouth and ask for it.

It took me even more years to learn that certain ways to ask for things are much more effective than others. That's something we're going to look at in a later chapter.

Why Many Don't Have Natural Self-Confidence

Millions of people were raised by people who were not living the life they really wanted, which means that they unknowingly passed that experience on to their children.

For example, when I was a kid, I would listen to how adults talked about their lives. Often I would hear adults talk about how much they regretted things they did or didn't do and how most of them seemed pretty unhappy.

It struck me, even as a kid, that most of the adults I met didn't seem very happy, and I always wondered why. Over time, I developed a theory that most adults aren't really living the lives that they want to live, and that they had somehow "settled" and taken whatever life had given to them.

Then these adults would love to lecture us kids about what *we* should do with our lives! I remember sitting there thinking, "Why the heck should I listen to your advice about how to live *my* life when you aren't even living the life *you* want?"

It wasn't until I became an adult myself that I learned a painful truth about life: things don't always work out the way you plan. Sometimes you work really hard for something, and it just doesn't go the way you hoped for.

After studying all those personal growth programs, I realized something that I don't think the adults I grew up with knew: it's not what happens to you, it's how you *respond* to what happens to you that makes all the difference.

IT'S NOT WHAT HAPPENS TO YOU, IT'S HOW YOU RESPOND TO WHAT HAPPENS TO YOU.

We've all heard of people who were born with what most of the world would call physical challenges but who went on to live amazing lives. Or people who have suffered devastating losses but built their lives back from the ground up.

Why do these stories inspire us? Because each of us has so much to be thankful for, yet we tend to ignore what we have and focus on what we don't have. That's why one of the big lessons of the Power Habits of Unstoppable Self-Confidence is to stop focusing on what you don't have, and instead focus your mind on what you do have—because when you do that, you'll get more of the experience of having.

Five Myths about Self-Confidence

Speaking of focus, let's now turn to the second question that my coaching clients often ask me: "What are some of the most common myths about self-confidence?"

Here are five of the most common myths— and with each one, I'm also going to give you the translation of what people are really saying when they bring them up.

These translations are examples of what I call *head trash*. Head trash is the negative voice in your head that tells you, "I can't do this," "You're not good enough," or negative messages like that. You can learn more about head trash in my books such as *Get Rid of Your Head Trash about Money.*

Each of us has different versions of head trash telling us why we're not enough of this or too much of that. Head trash is one of the main reasons why so many of us don't have natural self-confidence.

EACH OF THESE MYTHS IS A RESULT OF HEAD TRASH.

Here are five of the most common myths about self-confidence and their respective head trash translations:

Self-Confidence Myth 1: You've either got it or you don't.

Head trash translation: *"I wasn't born with self-confidence, so I'll probably never have it."*

As with most myths, there is a grain of truth to this. From my studies and interviews of over 250 millionaires and multimillionaires, I have learned that there apparently is a select group of people, whom I call the *naturals*, who did seem to pop out of the womb with natural self-confidence.

But if self-confidence was something that you either have at birth or you'll never have, you wouldn't be reading this book right now! Because I don't know of anyone who had less natural self-confidence than me. I am living proof that anyone, no matter what their background or circumstances, can develop self-confidence—provided that you are serious about it and willing to make some simple changes in your life.

So much for myth 1. Now let's go to the next one.

Self-Confidence Myth 2: The key to self-confidence is "Fake it 'til you make it."

Head trash translation: *"I have no idea what I'm doing, so I'll just smile and hope no one finds out that I don't know what I'm doing."*

Like the first myth, this has an element of truth to it. There are indeed times in life when we have to grin and bear it, hoping things will turn out all right even though we feel that we're in way over our heads.

For example, when I was going into the studio to record my first audio learning program, I was scared that I would mess it up and sound like a complete idiot. But I kept breathing and telling myself that everything was going to be fine. So you could argue that I faked it.

However—and I think this is the key to why this myth can really trip people up—long before I ever walked into that recording studio, I had done my homework. I had already written nine books on personal growth and success and had testimonials and success stories from over 1,000 people from around the world. Even though I felt scared of messing it up, I had done the research and preparation to be ready for that moment, and that's why I succeeded.

If I had tried to fake it in the literal sense and walked into the studio with no idea what I was going to say, or no proof or system to back up my claims, it would have been a very short session!

Legendary basketball coach Bobby Knight said it best: "The key to being a champion is NOT 'the will to win.' Everyone has that. What makes a champion is the will to PREPARE to win."

THE WILL TO PREPARE TO WIN MAKES A CHAMPION.

Self-Confidence Myth 3: Confidence comes naturally to talented people.

Head trash translation: *"I don't feel that confident, so I must not be very talented."*

This very dangerous myth stops many talented and creative people from taking action and following their dreams. The fact is, millions of creative, talented people don't have much self-confidence and therefore, don't follow their dreams. Conversely, there are also millions of people who aren't very talented, who believe they're God's gift to humanity!

This creates what I call "the TV talent show syndrome." Have you ever watched one of those TV talent shows where they have singers or acrobats or musical groups? What always amazes me is that often the artists who are the most talented are the quietest, shyest ones—whereas the loud, obnoxious ones who think they're the greatest thing in the world couldn't hold a tune if it had a handle on it!

It is definitely *not* true that all talented people have high self-confidence. In fact, it's often people with the *most* talent who have the *least* self-confidence.

MANY TALENTED PEOPLE HAVE LOW SELF-CONFIDENCE.

Nevertheless, it is not always talent that wins the day, but the person who has the courage and self-confidence to step up to the mic and belt out their song!

Self-Confidence Myth 4: If I'm nervous in social situations, it means I'm not self-confident.

Head trash translation: *"I don't know what to do or say in social settings, so I mostly avoid them so I don't embarrass myself."*

The fear of embarrassment is definitely one of the most common fears when it comes to self-confidence. Millions of us feel nervous when meeting new people because we're afraid that other people will judge us.

Well, let me you in on a little secret, one that helped me get over my own social anxiety: people are far too busy worrying about themselves to worry about judging you!

Naturally, none of us wants to look stupid or be made a fool of in front of other people. That's why, in a later chapter, we're going to specifically tackle this thorny issue of what to do and say in social settings and networking events so you'll never have to avoid them.

And don't worry: it doesn't involve anything like putting a lampshade on your head or trying to be the life of the party or pretending to be something you're not.

After trying dozens of different techniques and listening to all different kinds of teachers discuss human behavior in social settings, I finally came up with my own simple but highly effective method that will allow *anyone*, no matter how quiet or shy you are, to overcome social anxiety and let your true self shine through in any social setting.

Self-Confidence Myth 5: If I were smarter, better-looking, taller, thinner, richer (or whatever), I'd be more self-confident. Head trash translation: *"I'm not smart, attractive, tall, thin, rich, or fill-in-the-blank enough, so I'll never be really self-confident."*

Aha. Now we are getting to the root of the entire issue. The essential belief that is holding us back from being truly self-confident is the belief that "I'm not enough."

When I launched my coaching company, SuccessClinic.com, in 1997, the title of my first online newsletter was "You Are Enough." That's because I realized that this very belief—that "I'm not enough"—is the cause of almost every emotional pain, frustration, and handicap that causes us to hold ourselves back.

IF YOU BELIEVE YOU'RE NOT ENOUGH, YOU'LL ACT AS THOUGH IT'S TRUE.

Think about it. Let's say you really believe that you're not tall enough, and that's why you're not very self-confident. How are you going to behave if you really believe that? You're going to believe that other people are judging you based on your height. You might even call yourself "vertically challenged!"

If you're single, you probably won't go up to that attractive person at the party because you'll think, "Ahh, they probably won't like me because I'm not tall enough." You gave yourself an excuse to *not* take action. But can you see what's really going on here?

You have a convenient excuse for not taking action; therefore you will keep *not* taking action—which means you will not get the results you want in life, which will reinforce your own belief: "See? If only I were taller, I'd get the results I want."

It reminds me of an old Peanuts cartoon. Peppermint Patty is talking to her friend Marcie. Peppermint Patty says, "When you have a big nose, there's nothing you can do about it. See Marcie, I got an F on this paper! I know it's because I have a big nose." Marcie looks at Peppermint Patty's paper and says, "But sir, this paper is blank. You didn't write anything on it." And Peppermint Patty says, "See, when you have a big nose, there's nothing you can do about it!"

Peppermint Patty believed she wouldn't get a good grade, so she didn't even try! She handed in a blank paper, so of course she got an F. Yet her head trash was telling her the whole time, "I can't succeed because I've got a big nose, so why even try?"

As a result of this head trash, she didn't take any action because she figured, "Ah, what's the use?" Then used her excuse of having a big nose to explain her "failure!"

DON'T LET YOUR HEAD TRASH STOP YOU FROM TAKING ACTION.

How Head Trash Shows Up in Your Life

Yes, I realize that it's just a comic strip. But how many of us are doing something like this to ourselves every single day?

We tell ourselves, "I'm not as successful as I want to be because I'm not smart enough, not tall enough, not young enough, not attractive enough, not _____ enough."

Because we're listening to that head trash, and because we believe it to be true, we use it as a convenient excuse to avoid getting in the game and giving ourselves a chance to win.

How Much Is Your Head Trash Costing You Right Now?

This is a very important question: *If you don't learn how to take out your head trash, how much do you think it's going to cost you over the next 12 months?*

I want you to get a real number in your head as you read this. In fact, make a written note right now of the amount of money it's going to cost you if you don't take out your head trash in the next 12 months.

I ask this question of each of my clients whether we're doing one-on-one or group coaching. Let me give you a real-life example. I was talking with one of my clients, named Charles. I said, "Charles, how much do you think it's going to cost you over the next 12 months if you don't get this problem fixed, if we don't take out your head trash?"

Without batting an eye, he replied, "A million dollars. Noah, if I don't take out my head trash, I'm easily going to lose out on a million dollars in the next 12 months."

HEAD TRASH WAS COSTING CHARLES $1 MILLION A YEAR.

"This is very common," I said. "I talk to people every day who tell me that their head trash is costing them anywhere from $10,000 to $100,000 per month, or more—*and that adds up to losing six or seven figures each and every year!*

"Tell you what," I said. "Just give me 10 percent of that $1 million, and I'll find you that $1 million in the next 12 months. In other words, if you give me $1 and I give you $10 back, is that a good deal?"

"Yes, that's a very good deal."

So he did it—he paid me 10 percent of $1 million, or $100,000, to coach him one-on-one for the next 12 months. (I love coaching high achievers because they make decisions quickly and firmly, without delay.) Can you guess what happened next?

Turns out, I didn't find Charles a million dollars in the next 12 months. *I found him an additional $1.8 million dollars in just 10 months!*

Because of our one-on-one coaching, I found him nearly *$2 million* that he would have lost out on if he hadn't followed my advice and taken out his head trash. Talk about a breakthrough!

Moreover, because I helped him win his life back, Charles bought a new RV and went on a seven-week vacation with his wife. He told me that not only was he making more money than ever, he now has more time freedom than ever before. Now that's a win-win-win!

Common Symptoms of Head Trash

You could say that I've written more than twenty books about this one topic: how to take out your head trash. So let's look at some of the most common symptoms of head trash. Can you relate to any of these?

- Procrastination
- Low self-esteem
- Lack of self-confidence
- Negative self-talk
- Limiting beliefs
- Difficulty making decisions
- Fear of failure or rejection
- Perfectionism

- Difficulty managing time or setting priorities
- Difficulty taking action or following through on plans
- Difficulty with managing stress or life's challenges
- Trouble setting and achieving goals
- Difficulty in finding meaning or purpose in life
- Difficulty with feeling fulfilled or satisfied with life
- Struggling to maintain a healthy work-life balance
- Struggling with finding or pursuing your passion
- Difficulty finding happiness or contentment

Fact is, I struggled with almost all of these symptoms before I discovered my Inner Game Breakthrough Formula.

What *Won't* Fix the Problem

While most people aren't even aware of the problem, let alone how to fix it, let me share with you what *won't* fix this underlying problem that's causing all your other problems:

- Ignoring it or hoping it will go away on its own
- Trying to suppress or push down negative thoughts and feelings
- Believing head trash is a permanent part of your identity

- "Shelf-help" books or online courses
- Seeking quick fixes or shortcuts rather than addressing the root causes
- Vision boards
- Years of therapy
- Watching YouTube videos for hours on end
- Working harder and longer without a proven, plug-and-play solution that fixes the real problem.

How many of these have you tried without success?

Ten Types of Head Trash That Don't Serve You

These commonly held beliefs will *not* serve you:

1. "I'm not capable of overcoming my head trash."
2. "I don't have the time or resources to work on taking out my head trash."
3. "I'm too old to change."
4. "My head trash is a permanent part of me, and I just have to live with it."
5. "I'm not worthy or deserving of overcoming my head trash."
6. "I don't have the willpower or discipline to make changes."
7. "I don't have the support or resources I need to overcome my head trash."

8. "I'm too stuck in my ways to change."
9. "I'm too afraid of failure or rejection."
10. "Seeking help is a sign of weakness."

Do you believe any of these?

You have done all of these things in your life because you *believe* what you've been telling yourself. I want you to see just how these beliefs have affected your life—even though until this very moment you've probably been unaware of it. That means you're actually a very powerful manifestor.

Now let's examine the difference between *character* and *personality* and discover how to be yourself in a world that often doesn't support you for doing that.

2

Character versus Personality: How to Be Yourself in a World That Doesn't Want You to Be

Sow a thought, reap an action; sow an action,
reap a habit; sow a habit, reap a character;
sow a character, reap a destiny.
—STEPHEN R. COVEY

In 1992, I was one of the unhappiest people in the city of Los Angeles. Four years earlier, I had driven my 1977 Buick Riviera across the country from Maine to California to pursue my dream of becoming a movie star. Notice that I didn't say, "to be an actor"—because I really didn't care about the craft of acting. My only thought was about being a movie star, and I thought about it day and night.

Unfortunately, after arriving in Hollywood, I soon found out that the producers who were in charge of casting the movie roles that I so desperately wanted kept insisting that I do this irritating thing called "be a good actor." I responded with, "What?! Don't know you who I *am*?!"

Although it sounds funny when looking back on it, it was anything but funny back then. I was living in a cramped little one-bedroom apartment, and strangely enough, my mean old landlord was terribly insistent about the fact that I had to do this annoying thing called *paying rent* every month. What *was* it with these people?

Since those dumb Hollywood producers kept being underwhelmed by my incredible performances, I soon realized that I would have to find some kind of gainful employment in order to keep a roof over my head and food in my stomach.

I mentally went through a list of everything I was good at that could lead to gainful employment, and that added up to—nothing. I realized that I'd better think of something fast or that mean old landlord was going to put me and my belongings out on the street. (By the way, my "mean old landlord" was actually anything but—he let me be late on my rent more times than I could count. But I had no clue how to make the money that he kept insisting I pay him for the privilege of renting his apartment!)

I finally decided to go to a temp agency and learn how to use computers. Now this was back in the early 1990s, when floppy disks were actual disks that were floppy, and a having a lot of memory meant 128 kilobytes.

Nevertheless, hunger is the mother of persistence, so I persisted and taught myself how to use all those newfangled software programs like Lotus 123 and Windows 2.0. The temp agency saw that I was hungry and determined, so they kept sending me out on different assignments where I would work as a secretary—ahem, administrative assistant.

There was just one teeny little problem. I hated my job. No, I hated my *life*. I hated living in a cramped little one-bedroom apartment. I hated having barely enough money to cover my rent and eat in the same month. I hated coming home from work that I hated to my lonely apartment that I hated every night, feeling sick to my stomach. And I hated waking up the next morning, feeling as if someone had their hands around my throat.

I WAS THE PERSON CHOKING THE LIFE OUT OF ME.

Every morning on the way to work, I would feel as though someone were choking the life out of me. Yet the saddest part was that I knew the person choking the life out of me was me.

What Happened to All My Dreams?

Here I was, the guy who was going to take the world by storm—and all the dreams that I had had back in my college days had turned into nightmares. Was this life? Was this all I had to look forward to for the rest of my days on earth—working at a job I hated, barely making enough to make ends meet, being alone and lonely, living in fear and poverty—the very things I had driven over 3,000 miles to get away from?

In my heart, I longed for the ability to change people's lives, to make a difference, to have a platform upon which to change the world and leave a legacy. Yet I had no idea what I was supposed to do with the rest of my life, let alone how to do it.

Then, in the fall of 1992, a friend of mine told me about a church he was attending and how the minister there was a really good speaker. When I was growing up, I had been raised in a church that told me that I was a sinner, and nothing I did would ever be good enough. (Working as a professional ballet dancer certainly helped to reinforce that belief, since nothing I did *was* ever good enough!) That's why I was approximately as excited about going back to church as a turkey is about Thanksgiving Day. However, for some strange reason, I decided to give it a try.

I walked into that church, the North Hollywood Church of Religious Science, and heard the minister talk about the nature of God and man.

The minister said, "There is no spot where God is not."

He said, "God and you are one."

He said, "God is right where you are."

I had never heard such things spoken out loud before.

I had been raised to believe that God was some old white guy with a long beard who didn't like me, didn't approve of me, and would never be happy with me or what I did. I had never heard of the idea that God could actually be *right here where I am* . . . and could actually *approve of* me!

> **THIS WAS THE BEGINNING OF MY SPIRITUAL AWAKENING.**

The Foundation of My Spiritual Awakening

I started taking classes at the church and learning about the teachings of Dr. Ernest Holmes, the founder of the Church of Religious Science (the Science of Mind). I started studying other metaphysical teachers, like Louise Hay, Catherine Ponder, and Deepak Chopra.

For the first time in my life, I learned how to pray and began meditating and journaling, learning how to quiet my mind and listen to God. I know that sounds awfully woo-woo to some people, but please understand that up until that point in my life, I had been so cut off from my own feelings that I would just go along with whatever anyone else told me to do. *It was the first time I had ever asked myself what I really wanted.*

One day, I was meditating when I decided to ask God what he wanted me to do with the rest of my life. I'm not sure what I was expecting, but what happened next was the last thing I expected.

After I asked the question, I heard a voice say, *Move back to Maine.* The voice came from inside in my head, but the words were as clear as any that had ever been spoken out loud to me.

After I heard the words, *Move back to Maine,* my next thought was, *Are you kidding me?*

WHEN I HEARD THAT VOICE, I THOUGHT, "ARE YOU KIDDING ME?"

I hadn't lived in New England for nearly a decade, and moving back there was the last thing I wanted to do. I decided that it was a stupid idea and to ignore that voice, whoever it was—because whoever it was was clearly insane.

Yet every time I began to pray or meditate, the voice would come back into my head: *Move back to Maine.* In fact, if the story of my life were ever made into a movie, it would be *Conversations with God meets Field of Dreams!*

Trying to Ignore My Inner Voice

The more I tried to ignore the voice, the more I realized that it simply wasn't going away. It kept saying the same thing over and over again.

Have you ever had something like that happen to you? Maybe not in the form of an actual voice, but an inner knowing or prompting that doesn't make any logical sense, so you try to ignore it or push it down. Well, that's what I tried to do.

However, as I began to journal, pray, and meditate about it, it dawned on me that I really didn't want to live in Los Angeles any more and that my time there had served its purpose. I finally decided to do something that made absolutely no sense. I sold my car, my furniture, and most of my belongings, bought a one-way plane ticket, and moved back to Maine.

Once I got there, I began working with a business mentor—a highly skilled coach who helped me better understand how I could use my talents and skills to make a difference and make money.

With my mentor's support and guidance, I decided to go back to college to finish my degree. In college for the second time, I decided to major in religious studies and thought I'd end up as a college professor, or even a minister.

And that's how I came to be in that college dorm room on April 24, 1997, experience the Shower That Changed Everything and discovered my AFFORMATIONS® Method—the exact method that has changed over a million lives around the world for more than twenty-five years.

THIS IS HOW THE RIGHT COACH OR MENTOR CAN CHANGE YOUR LIFE.

That discovery led to the publication of my first book, *Permission to Succeed.* Then people started hiring me to coach them to get better results in their lives, businesses, careers, and relationships.

Then my coaching clients began getting amazing results—like making more in just 12 weeks than they had made in the previous 12 months, while winning their lives back.

Then I started sharing my experience in my other books, online courses, keynote speeches, private workshops, and one-on-one and group coaching programs.

As I published more books, I started crisscrossing the country again, this time doing keynote speeches and leading workshops for Fortune 500 companies and national associations. I had finally discovered what I was here on earth to do.

One month after my fortieth birthday, I moved to a little town in northeast Ohio. Before I moved there, I'm not sure that I could have pointed to the state of Ohio on a map of the United States. But a friend persuaded me to relocate there, because he lived there and said it would be—and I'm quoting here—"fun."

Okaaaaaay . . .

Three weeks after I moved to Ohio—knowing only one person, the friend who convinced me to move there—that friend introduced me to one of his friends, who in turn introduced me to this gorgeous blonde named Babette.

A short time later, I got up the courage to ask her to go ballroom dancing with me, because I figured if I could take her dancing, maybe I'd sweep her off her feet. It turns out that I was the one who was swept off my feet!

Babette and I were married on April 30, 2011. At our wedding, in front of family and friends, I gave her this toast: "Because you loved me for who I am, you made me want to be a better man." And I was crying when I said it!

THIS IS HOW YOUR LIFE CAN CHANGE IN UNEXPECTED WAYS.

The years since I turned forty have been the happiest of my life, because in Babette, I finally found the person who sees me and believes in me, and makes me believe I can do more than I think I can do.

Character Ethic versus Personality Ethic

During this time, I discovered the teachings of Stephen Covey, author of *The 7 Habits of Highly Effective People*. When I first heard Dr. Covey's work, it touched me very deeply. In fact, the first time I listened to *The 7 Habits* audio recording, I realized that for my whole life, I had been doing "The 7 Habits of Highly INEFFECTIVE People."

One thing that affected me deeply about Dr. Covey's work was his discussion of the *character ethic* and the *personality ethic*. His work was based on his study of the success literature published in the United States from 1776 to 1976. As he states, for the first 150 years, most of the success literature published in this country focused on the character ethic. Things like integrity, humility, simplicity, fairness, modesty, fidelity, courage, justice, and the Golden Rule were seen as the foundation of success.

But after World War I, the basic view of success shifted from the character ethic to the *personality ethic*. These new books contended the driving force behind success was an individual's personality—their public image, what they did, and how they performed in social interactions—a positive mental attitude as well as skills and techniques to get people to behave in certain ways.

While some of this newer literature briefly discussed the importance of character, it became mostly lip service—meaning that as long as you say and do the right things and package yourself in the right way, you will be likely to get the results you want.

Naturally, since I was born in the late 1960s, I had had virtually no experience with the success literature from the earlier era of character. Instead, I had been raised on a steady diet of the personality ethic. All the success books I had ever encountered said that you should smile, dress nicely, say and do the right things, and if you appear interested in other people, you can get what you want in life.

After I heard Dr. Covey discuss the difference between the character ethic and the personality ethic, I finally realized what had been missing my whole adult life: I had unknowingly been taught to manipulate, control, and maneuver my way through life without ever taking into account who I really was or what I actually wanted to do.

It occurred to me that this was the height of irony—all those self-help books and programs had been telling us that *this is the way* to get what you want in life. The not-so-hidden message in all of these programs is clear: "Fake it until you make it." They're really saying, "You can be false, and it doesn't matter. You can fake people out, and it doesn't matter. It doesn't matter who you are; just make other people *like you*, and they'll give you want you want most of the time."

> **THE BIGGEST IRONY OF ALL THOSE SELF-HELP BOOKS I'D BEEN READING: THEY WERE TEACHING "FAKE IT TILL YOU MAKE IT."**

Wow.

That was a stunning realization for me. I was shocked to realize that while I had been mostly faking my way through life (because I had no idea who I was or what I really wanted), I had also been manipulated by many people. They had done exactly the same thing to me, because we'd all been reading the same books!

Restoring the Character Ethic

All I had ever tried to do was *change my personality*—change who I was to get what I wanted. Why had I done that? Because I assumed I *had to* change who I was in order to get what I wanted. That was what all these gurus told me I had to do in order to succeed. I had never heard anyone talk about character, how important it is, or even that you should have it at all.

As I have been teaching people around the world for more than two decades now, I see more and more how important it is to restore the character ethic to our lives and our society.

What Is Character?

What is character, why is it so important, and how can we develop it if we've had such little training in it for, oh, these past 100 years or so?

The word *character* comes from an ancient Greek word meaning *engraved mark*, *symbol*, or *imprint* and can be traced even further back to the words for *to engrave* and *to scrape and scratch*. In ancient times, a *character* was the stamp or marking impressed into wax and clay. It served as the signature or monogram of the artist or inventor who created unique works of art.

In the seventeenth century, the word *character* came to mean the sum of qualities that define a person. These include a person's thoughts, ideas, motives, judgment, behavior, imagination, and emotions. In

1908, William Straton Bruce wrote in *The Formation of Christian Character:* "All of these components go to the shaping and coloring of a person's character. They all have some part in producing that final type of self, that ultimate habit of will, into which a person's whole activities at last shape themselves."

All of us seem to have a sense of what *character* means and why it's so important. Yet the question for many people today is: "Why bother to develop character in today's modern world when every day you see people who *don't* have character get ahead and become wildly successful?"

It's true: every day, the media are filled with celebrities who have done nothing but, for example, appear on a reality TV show—meaning that they have become famous simply because millions of people are watching them on TV. They are indeed famous for being famous.

THIS IS WHY CHARACTER STILL MATTERS.

The Reality Show Syndrome

This phenomenon—what I call the *reality show syndrome*—is the perfect example of the difference between the character ethic and the personality ethic.

It takes no character whatsoever to appear on a reality show. In fact, the producers of these shows encourage the worst possible behavior from the people who appear on these shows, because it makes for higher ratings!

In a recent survey conducted by the Pew Research Center, 81 percent of eighteen- to twenty-five-year-olds surveyed said that *getting rich* is their generation's most important or second most important life goal; 51 percent said the same about *being famous.*

According to David Morrison of the Philadelphia-based research firm Twentysomething Inc., "We're seeing the common person become famous for being themselves." He says: "Look at *Big Brother* and other shows. People being themselves can be incredibly famous and get sponsorship deals, and become celebrities. It's a completely new development in entertainment, and it's having a crossover effect on attitudes and behavior."

The media's constant force-feeding of images of glamour and excess to our TV screens is helping to create a new generation of young people whose major life goals are getting rich and being famous. Is it any wonder that we've gotten to this point after nearly 100 years of a steady diet of the personality ethic, where having a good character could hardly matter less?

Why, then, are we surprised or shocked when we read stories about celebrities acting out and causing trouble, getting arrested for drunk driving and other reckless behavior—when every day society is telling them that they have reached the pinnacle of success?

With all of this as the new reality, how can we restore the character ethic and develop character in a world that seems not to value it or even care about it?

The Main Difference between Character and Personality

It seems to me that the answer lies in the very difference between character and personality. We react with shock when celebrities behave badly, yet our modern world is set up to revere celebrity as the be-all, end-all goal in itself—to be rich and famous rather than having done something worthwhile or contributing something positive to society.

One of the downsides about being a celebrity is that there is no one to say no to you. As such, the celebrity doesn't have anyone who sets boundaries and says, "You know, that might not be such a great idea."

When celebrities become rich and famous, they surround themselves with a phalanx of yes-men and enablers who give them everything they want and allow them to get away with whatever they want. No one's going to say no to that celebrity, because if you're a yes-man, that celebrity is your meal ticket. Imagine for a moment that you're one of the biggest celebrities in the world.

THIS IS WHY BEING A CELEBRITY ISN'T ALWAYS EASY.

Who is going to tell you no? Who among your retinue of yes-men is ever going to say, "Um, dude, you might not want to do that"?

When there's no one to say no to you, why would you ever say no to yourself?

Perhaps that's the foundation of character—the ability to say no to yourself, the habit of making the right choices even when it's easy to make the wrong ones.

I believe we all know the difference between right and wrong. We know it's wrong to lie, cheat, and steal. We know it's right to give value, serve a higher purpose, and tell the truth even when the truth is painful. Yet it's easy to lose sight of these things and take the fast and easy route to success, especially in today's society, which values money and fame above all else.

But when you get rich and famous without character, fame and riches may not last long. In any case, you may very well find them to be empty and meaningless. This is why there are so many stories of celebrities who have lost their way (and even their lives) after becoming rich and famous. It's so common that it's become a cliché.

I'm not suggesting that there's anything wrong with being rich and famous. But a person's character is the foundation upon which the house of self-confidence and success is built. If you don't have a strong foundation, you're building your house on sand, and it won't stand the test of time.

How to Develop Character in a World That Doesn't Value It

How can you develop character in a world that doesn't seem to value it? How can you increase your self-confidence in a world that keeps telling you to fake it until you make it? Here are three simple things you can do, starting right now, to develop character, even in today's modern world.

1. Practice the habit of daily journaling.

Every morning when you wake up, make it a habit to write one to three pages in your journal. Why is journaling so important? There is something mystical and powerful about asking yourself what you really think and setting them to paper.

Many years ago, when I first started daily journaling, I would fill page after page after page with my thoughts and feelings. For my whole life, I had been so out of touch with my own feelings and opinions that I really didn't know what I thought about anything. Because I wasn't listening to my own inner knowing and intuition, I trusted the wrong people, made poor decisions, and had very low self-confidence.

It wasn't until I made it a habit to write down every day what I was thinking and feeling that I started to make better choices in the moment of decision. As a result, I found myself becoming more and more self-confident, believing that I had a right to state my own opinion and speak my mind, even if someone else didn't agree with me. That in turn empowered me to make better decisions based on my own beliefs, not what someone else told me I should think.

2. Practice the habit of daily meditation.

Meditation is simply the practice of quieting your mind and shutting out all the distractions of the world. As I often say to my clients, we don't live in the Information Age; we live in the Information Overload Age.

What if you've never meditated before? How can you start doing it? It doesn't have to be complicated.

First, sit in either a comfortable chair or, if you prefer, sit cross-legged on the floor or on a comfortable mat, like a yoga mat.

Next, become aware of your breath. Focus your mind on your breathing, in and out. Count one, two, three, on the inhale, hold for a count of three, then breathe out one, two, three.

Then become aware of your thoughts. Invariably you will start to go through your laundry list of all the things you have to do that day, and all the things pressing on you that have to get done: *"Remember to pick up the dry cleaning. We need milk and eggs. I've gotta write that report,"* and things like that.

I recommend that you (and I do this all the time when I'm meditating) keep your notepad and pen within arm's reach. When your laundry list thoughts start to come up (which they invariably will), simply take out your pen and paper, and write them down.

Pretty soon, your mind will run out of things to remind you of! You'll be left with nothing to think about and nothing to remember. What do you do then?

Your mind is probably used to thinking, thinking, thinking of all the things you have to do today. That's why it's so important to get these things out of your head and capture them on paper.

3. Practice the habit of saying thank you.

My daily mantra is simply those two words: "Thank you."

I say, "Thank you" in my mind and I think about my health.

I say, "Thank you" in my mind and I think about my fingers and toes and arms and legs and the fact that I can walk around and feel and touch and smell and see and hear.

THANK YOU: THE TWO MOST IMPORTANT WORDS YOU CAN SAY EVERY DAY.

I say, "Thank you" in my mind and I think about the fact that I have a beautiful wife, an amazing home, food in my refrigerator, money in the bank, friends, family, and all the other things that I'm grateful for.

I say, "Thank you" in my mind, and I think about all the treasures and beauty of this magnificent planet earth—the beaches and sky and flowers and trees and animals, and all the beauty that's all around us every moment of every day.

I say "Thank you" for all the gifts of my life—and instantly I feel better. I feel at peace. I feel grateful and humbled to be who I am and where I am and to have so much to be grateful for.

Can you see how taking just a few moments to say thank you every day can—indeed, must—change your life?

Right now, your head trash might be saying, *"This sounds amazing, but I'm worried that I won't see any progress or results."*

Here's what Aubrey, one of my clients, says about coaching with me:

When I first attended a Noah St. John event, I came thinking, "How can Noah figure out things about me? I'm different than anyone else, and I don't think these things will come up." But the things Noah says bring up ideas and thoughts in your mind to where you learn that much more about yourself.

Now everybody comes from different walks of life, different businesses, different issues, different things that they're stuck in, different head trash, as Noah calls it. And he has a way of engaging everybody. It doesn't matter where you're stuck; I'm able to learn more and grow more. Before you even realize it, he's taught you how to make more money, and you don't even realize how it happened! I know that happened with me. And it was simply before I even really started working his habits into my business, it was really getting rid of the head trash, as he teaches. And as I did that, *within a year, my business income that I had actually had for 15 years had DOUBLED* simply by incorporating the habits that Noah teaches.

The fact is, there's no better time than right now. It seems inconvenient initially, but then once you've done it, you're like, "I can't imagine having had missed that and not having that peace in my life."

Have you heard the phrase *working yourself to death*? Aubrey had been doing that before she came to me. It's true: she told me that she had been working 100 or more hours every week for 15 years. She was working so hard that she ended up in a wheelchair, and her doctors told her that she might never walk again. They told her that she had to stop working so hard. But she couldn't, because she was on a treadmill and just working, working, working all the time.

When she first came to one of my events, she was at her lowest point. Yet because of my coaching and her implementation, *she doubled her income in just 12 months, after 15 years of nearly working herself to death.*

Many people will read Aubrey's story and the other

AUBREY WAS LITERALLY WORKING HERSELF TO DEATH.

case studies in this book or on my website and say to themselves, "Sure, they did it, but it won't work for me."

What does that sound like to you? Exactly: *More head trash!*

So I want you to reverse that right now. Instead of believing that old head trash, I want you to start saying this: **If they did it, why not me?**

Is it ridiculous to think that just one thing I've taught you so far in this book could help you get better results in the next 12 weeks?

I hope you agree that it's not ridiculous at all. In fact, it's perfectly logical, right?

Here's All You Need to Succeed

The only three things you need to succeed are:

1. The right PLAN (what to do)
2. The right TOOLS (how to do it)
3. The right SUPPORT (the people who believe in you)

Building your dream business, dream career, and dream lifestyle is like building your dream home. First, you need *the right PLAN:* the blueprint you're going to follow. In my coaching programs, that involves the paint-by-numbers, fill-in-the-blanks, plug-and-play systems, templates, resources, and strategies that have made billions for my clients and me over the last two decades plus.

Then you need *the right TOOLS* that enable you to actually build the business or lifestyle you desire.

Finally, you need *the right SUPPORT*. You need the person or people in your corner believing in you— often before you even believe in yourself!

In my one-on-one and group coaching programs like the Inner Game Breakthrough, we call these the three pillars of transformation: the *right plan*, the *right tools*, and the *right support*, so you reach your pot of gold faster than you ever could by working alone.

Let me end this chapter with a quote from actor Denzel Washington:

I've found that nothing in life is worthwhile unless you take risks. Nothing. Nelson Mandela said, "There is no passion to be found playing small and settling for a life that's less than the one you're capable of living." Without consistency, you'll never finish. So do what you feel passionate about. Take chances. Don't be afraid to fail big, to dream big. But remember, dreams without goals are just dreams.

Let me add that a goal without action is just a dream. You can have all the big dreams in the world, but if you don't take action, nothing will happen!

In our next chapter, I'll walk you through a simple but highly effective method that will help you change your beliefs, your habits, and your life. Let's go!

3

How to Take Control
of Your Habits

Never bend your head. Always hold it high.
Look the world straight in the eye.

—HELEN KELLER

Once upon a time, there was a young man who was shy, soft-spoken, and only a mediocre student at school. At the age of eighteen, he left his native India and traveled to England to study the bar and become a lawyer.

Upon arriving in England, the young man attempted to fit into English society—buying new suits, fine-tuning his English accent, learning French, and taking violin and dance lessons.

After three months of these expensive endeavors, the young man decided they just weren't for him. He canceled all of these classes and spent the remainder of his three-year stay in London being a serious student and living a very simple lifestyle.

The young man successfully passed the bar on June 10, 1891, and sailed back to India two days later. For the next two years, he attempted to practice law there. Unfortunately, he found that he lacked both knowledge of Indian law and self-confidence at trial. When he was offered a year-long position to take a case in South Africa, he was grateful for the opportunity.

At age twenty-three, he once again left his family behind and set off for South Africa, arriving in British-governed Natal in May 1893. Although he was simply hoping to earn some money and learn more about the law, here this young man began his transformation from a quiet and shy person to one of the most respected leaders in history.

The seeds of this remarkable transformation were sown during a business trip shortly after his arrival in South Africa. The young man had only been there for about a week when he was asked to take the long trip from Natal to the capital of the Dutch-governed Transvaal province of South Africa for his case.

It was to be a several-day trip, including transportation by train and stagecoach. When the young man boarded the first train of his journey, railroad officials told him that he needed to transfer to the third-class passenger car. When the young man, who was holding first-class tickets, refused to move, a policeman came and threw him off the train.

This was not the last of the injustices that he suffered on this trip. In fact, as he spoke with other Indians in South Africa, he found that his experiences were not isolated incidents but were the norm.

During that first night of his trip, sitting in the cold of the railroad station after being thrown off the train, this young man contemplated whether he should go back home to India or fight the discrimination. After much thought, Mohandas Gandhi decided that he could not let these injustices continue—and that he was going to fight to change them.

Gandhi spent the next twenty years of his life working to better Indians' rights in South Africa. After that, he returned to India, where he became one of the most recognized and revered leaders in human history and was given the honorary title of Mahatma, which literally means *great soul*.

Mahatma Gandhi—someone who, throughout his entire life, considered himself a very ordinary person—transformed himself from someone who was too shy to speak in front of a group of people into one of the most influential leaders the world has ever known. How did he do it?

Whether he did it consciously or unconsciously, Gandhi—like many other people who have decided to transform their lives—followed the steps that I'll teach you in this program and ultimately mastered the Power Habits of Unstoppable Self-Confidence.

As we continue our journey of self-discovery, let's start with the question you may be asking right now: what are habits, how are they formed, and how can they be changed?

In my other books, such as *Power Habits* and *The 7-Figure Life,* I revealed how neuroscience is beginning to shed new light on the answers to these age-old questions. Keeping in mind how essential this knowledge is to our ability to understand and change our habits, let me offer a brief overview that will enable us to dive into these fundamental questions.

Neuroscience and Habits

Neuroscience, the study of the human brain and its function, is providing new insights into the relationship between habits, success, and self-confidence.

First of all, what is a habit? Simply put, a habit is *A tendency to act in a particular way in a particular situation.* It is a pattern of behavior a person typically performs in response to a given situation or set of circumstances.

Let's take a common situation. Let's say that you are going through your day, just like any other day, and at about three o'clock in the afternoon, you start to feel a little tired. Your eyes get a little droopy, you find it hard to focus on the project at hand, your body feels a little sluggish, and you lose some steam.

> **A HABIT IS A TENDENCY TO ACT IN A PARTICULAR WAY IN A PARTICULAR SITUATION.**

This happens because of the circadian rhythm or biological clock. Human beings, like most living creatures on earth, tend to be awake during the daytime and asleep during the night. Therefore our deepest sleep usually occurs between 2 and 4 a.m.

As a result, between the hours of two and four in the afternoon, our bodies are furthest in time from when our deepest sleep occurred the night before. That's why it's common for us to get a little sleepy during these hours.

For this reason, many European cultures, as well as companies as diverse as Google, Ben & Jerry's, and NASA, encourage their employees to take naps during work hours. These forward-thinking companies realize that napping has been shown to improve employee productivity and engagement.

Many people reach for a cup of coffee, a jolt of caffeine, a can of soda, or some other artificial stimulant to shock their bodies into getting through this sleepy period in the afternoon. If you are one of the millions of people who follow this pattern, you have developed the habit of using artificial stimulants to help you get through the day. Yet that's just part of the story.

The Big Picture

Neuroscience has revealed that the human brain developed in three separate stages. First came the old brain, or what is sometimes called the *reptile brain*. This part of the brain is responsible for our basic survival, including fight/flight/freeze responses. The reptile brain doesn't have a lot of thinking capacity, because it developed millions of years ago, long before our higher brain functions evolved.

Next comes the *midbrain*, which determines the meaning of things and social contexts. Finally, the *neocortex* evolved, with the ability to solve problems, think about complex issues, and produce answers using reason and logic.

THE REPTILE BRAIN IS THE MOST ANCIENT PART OF YOUR BRAIN.

According to scientific research, these three distinct parts of your brain work together but independently. To give you an idea of how this works in everyday life, imagine this scenario:

You are walking to your car, and suddenly someone starts shouting. What's your first reaction? It might be to jump and perhaps even feel a sense of fear. That is your reptile brain at work. You jump when something startles you because your reptile brain is wired directly to your muscles and makes your body instantly react *without your having to consciously think about it.*

For example, what happens when you accidentally touch a hot surface or something sharp? Do you sit there and think, "Gee, I should probably pull my hand away now, because this hurts"? No, you instinctively, without thinking about it, pull your hand away and yell, "Ouch!"

YOUR BRAIN'S NATURAL INSTINCTS CAUSE YOU TO REACT WITHOUT HAVING TO THINK.

This instinctual behavior—the natural instinct to protect your physical body and keep you out of harm's way—comes in handy when you are trying to outrun predators who would like to have you for dinner, literally!

To go back to our parking lot scenario, the next thing that happens is that after your initial jolt of fear, you will try to *understand* what's happening. In other words, your midbrain will attempt to make meaning from the situation. For example, it will quickly try to identify the person doing the yelling and placing him or her in a social context. Your midbrain will essentially ask itself: *"Do I know this person, or are they a stranger? Are they a friendly coworker or an angry parking lot attendant? Are they a threat to my safety, or will I be OK?"*

Finally, your neocortex, or problem-solving brain, will process the situation, and you figure it out: *"It's OK. It's just some guy calling to his buddy across the street."*

In short, our internal thought process exactly matches our evolution. Our first need is to survive. That is the job of the reptile brain—to keep us alive and take care of our basic survival needs. Then we develop social relationships. That is the area handled by the midbrain. Finally, we tackle problem-solving and the higher brain functions of the neocortex.

A Remarkably Efficient Machine

The brain is a remarkably efficient machine. Just as neuroscience has shown that the brain developed in these three separate but interrelated stages, it has also shown that your brain is wired so as to use the least amount of energy to accomplish the tasks it needs to do.

In the early 1990s, a group of scientists at the Massachusetts Institute of Technology ran a series of tests on the brains of rats in order to better understand the relationship between habits and brain function.

They hooked up a machine to measure rats' brain activity as they were placed into a maze that had a piece of chocolate at the opposite end. When each rat was released into the maze, the scientists observed that its brain became a flurry of activity. It was as if the brain were working overtime to try and discover where the treat at the end of the maze was.

What amazed the scientists was what happened when they put the same rats into the same maze with the same treats in the same place over and over again. As the rats learned where the chocolate was, their overall brain activity went down. Rather than having to figure it out from scratch, they began not only to remember but to use less brain activity to get there. They became creatures of habit.

The Habit Loop

This is where we come to what neuroscientists call the *habit loop*. As I showed in my other books, like *Power Habits,* the habit loop begins with three basic elements: the *cue*, the *routine*, and the *reward*. Let's look at how these elements work to create a habit and how this relates to self-confidence.

The first element is the *cue*. The cue is what happens when a stimulus or trigger comes either from the outside world—like someone yelling in a parking lot—or from your inside world, like getting sleepy around three in the afternoon. Every day you encounter hundreds, perhaps thousands, of cues. The sun comes up; you feel hungry;you feel tired; an email arrives in your inbox; the mailman arrives; you feel hungry again; and so on.

Each event is a cue that triggers your brain to do something. That "something" is the next element of the habit loop, and it's called the *routine*. The routine is what happens after the cue is triggered.

Let's take a simple habit like brushing your teeth. You reach for the toothbrush: that's the cue. Then you automatically put toothpaste on your toothbrush. If we were to look inside your brain at that moment, we would probably see very little activity in the area of your brain that's in charge of putting toothpaste on toothbrush. That's because you've done this process so many times before in your life that you do not think about it.

EVERY DAY, YOUR BRAIN RECEIVES THOUSANDS OF CUES.

Remember that the main job of your brain is survival. The reptile brain is vastly older and more instinctual than the midbrain or the neocortex. That's because our species' basic survival needs evolved millions of years before social relationships and the need for higher problem-solving.

The third element of the habit loop is the *reward*. Just like the rats in the maze, our human brain craves rewards for its activity. On a brain level, the reward is what happens after the cue is triggered and the routine is performed.

Let's look at an example from your everyday life that relates to your level of self-confidence and see how your brain reacts to it.

The Habit of Being More Organized

Let's say that you want to increase your self-confidence by getting more organized at work. In fact, one of the most common New Year's resolutions, in addition to losing weight and getting in shape, is to be more organized.

With the hectic pace of modern life, it's sometimes very hard to stay on top of everything but very easy to let things slide. So you have a desire to get organized—you *want* to do it—yet circumstances seem to be working against you.

The cue that appears could be any number of things: an email shows up in your inbox, the mailman arrives with the mail, someone puts a stack of papers on your desk, and so on.

Let's look at that stack of papers. When it hits your desk, what do you do with it?

Your neocortex or problem-solving brain will probably say something like this to you: *"You know, we really should organize those papers. Otherwise, they're going to fall into the black hole called 'my desk' along with all these other piles of paper we've got around here!"*

Your neocortex will try to logically reason with you, telling you *why* you should get organized and file those papers properly and immediately.

Meanwhile, your midbrain will probably be saying something like this: *"How important are these papers, really? Is it really that important to file these papers, or is there something else I should be doing right now?"*

Your midbrain will attempt to find the meaning and context of this new cue—a bunch of papers on your desk.

In the midst of all this, your reptile brain is thinking: *"Is this pile of papers going to attack me? Is it dangerous? Or can I just ignore it and still be all right?"*

Remember, your reptile brain's purpose is to keep you alive. Since it's unlikely that that pile of papers is going to jump up and assault you, your reptile brain tells the rest of your brain to ignore it. This is why your reptile brain so often wins this argument and leaves your midbrain and neocortex to fight it out between themselves.

THIS IS HOW YOUR BRAIN FIGHTS WITH ITSELF.

Can you see now why it's so easy to let those papers pile up and why it takes a huge amount of brain effort to file them and get organized?

Why Most New Year's Resolutions Fail

This is, in fact, the main reason that most people who set New Year's resolutions fail to keep them: you have been trying to change your habits using your willpower, which is your neocortex or logical brain, fighting that ancient, survival part of your brain that tells you to ignore the cue!

So what's the problem here? If it's not life and death, why should we change this habit—or any other one, for that matter? And how does all this relate to your level of self-confidence?

There's good news and bad news about your reptile brain. The good news is that it does a fantastic job of keeping you alive. It makes your body jump when there's a perceived danger, takes your hand off a hot surface in a split second, and many other amazing things that you never even have to think about.

The bad news about the reptile brain is that, as good as it is at keeping you alive, it has not really kept up with modern life. There are not many saber-toothed tigers running around today trying to kill you, but your reptile brain really isn't aware of that. It hasn't read the newspaper or turned on the TV in about five million years. It's just humming along, doing its job, as it has pretty much since dinosaurs roamed the earth.

THE REPTILE BRAIN HAS NOT KEPT UP WITH MODERN LIFE.

While your reptile brain has done a fantastic job in ensuring the survival of the human species, life today demands a lot more of our brains.

The Problem With Just Surviving

Your reptile brain is right: that pile of paper isn't going to jump up and attack you. The problem is, if you let that pile of paper just sit there, unfortunately it will soon be followed by another pile of paper, then another, and another, and another. Soon, you won't be able to see your desk, let alone get any work done. Ultimately, that will hurt your self-confidence.

Think of the crush of emails, reports, websites, text messages, blogs, information channels, and so on that most of us have to deal with every day. That's why it's vitally important to stay ahead of the curve and be proactive in staying organized.

In addition, with all the readily available junk food, it's incredibly easy to fall into the trap of mindlessly eating things that are bad for your health. That's why it's so important to develop the habit of eating right and exercising regularly if you want to increase your self-confidence.

But you knew all that already. Why then, is it so hard to change our habits and do the things we know we should be doing? The answer has to do with the next element of the habit loop—the one that neuroscientists call *craving*.

The Craving for Systems

Let me give you an example of how this works. I have always been a neat and orderly person. From the time I was very young, I enjoyed having everything in my room in nice, neat rows. In my early twenties, I even found myself working as a housekeeper at a five-star

CRAVINGS ARE KEY TO THE HABIT LOOP.

inn, and I actually enjoyed cleaning the rooms and keeping them in tip-top shape.

Later, after I started my own business and started to write books, hire employees, create websites, and so forth, life became often unpredictable. I realized that I would have to create *systems* to deal with the massive influx of information that was coming at me every day.

So I started to create systems to deal with requests to speak, customer service issues, and people contacting me to coach them. Sometimes it can seem overwhelming to have all of these cues coming at you every day. But in my brain, I developed a craving for the good feeling that comes from having a neat desk and an organized inbox.

Now some people would say that it doesn't sound like much fun to be so regimented. Yet I would argue that the very point of having these kinds of organizational systems is to allow you to be far more creative.

For example, as I was writing this book for you, I had to block out many hours each day for the time it took me to research, write, edit, and rewrite it. That would not have been possible if I did not have the other systems in place to keep my life and business running while I created this book.

My wife jokes about it to our friends. She'll say, "Noah has a system for everything, from how he gets dressed in the morning to how he takes out the trash." She's right!

Rather than trying to use your willpower to become more organized—or indeed to change any habit—there's a much simpler and easier way to do it.

Since being more organized will increase your level of self-confidence, you want to develop a *craving* for the feeling of being organized.

How do you do that? Well, let me ask you a question. Remember the last time you cleaned your desk or cleared out the clutter in your home or office? After letting the clutter pile up for so long, you probably got to the point where you said, "I can't take it any more!" And you decided to clean up, clear out, and even throw away a lot of stuff you found you didn't need any more.

Let me ask you: how did you feel after you had done that cleaning and clearing? I'd be willing to bet that you took a deep breath and said, "Whew! Wow, I feel *so* much better!"

YOU FEEL BETTER WHEN YOU CLEAR THE CLUTTER.

You feel better when you get organized because clutter in your environment make it much harder for good things to come in. And that's definitely going to harm your self-confidence.

From Totally Stuck to Regional Vice President in 12 Weeks

A coaching client joined my Inner Game Breakthrough program because she was a hard-working mom in the direct sales industry who had spent thousands of dollars on self-help and money-making programs, yet as hard as she worked, she just couldn't seem to get ahead. As a result, her self-confidence was very low.

As we began our coaching sessions, I asked her to tell me about her typical day. She said, "First, I go through my phone messages and see if has anyone placed an order. If someone has, I go upstairs to the bedroom and try to find my computer. Then I place the order."

"Wait a minute," I said. "Did you just say you go upstairs and *try* to find your computer?"

"Yes."

"What do you mean, *try* to find your computer?"

"My computer is upstairs in the bedroom, and it's usually buried under a pile of clothes or something."

"Do you think there might be a problem with that?"

"I've tried to get organized, but I can't seem to make it stick."

"Do you have kids?"

She said she did.

"Would you like your kids to have a nice lifestyle, go to college, and things like that?" I asked.

"Of course," she said.

"Well then," I said, "don't think of it as getting organized. Think of it as giving your kids a better future. You need to focus not on the doing of it, but the *result* of having gotten organized."

I gave her specific strategies to organize her workspace and separate her home life from her work life—starting with getting her computer out of the bedroom.

She took my advice and went from being totally stuck and having very little self-confidence to being promoted to regional vice president in her company in less than 12 weeks. Talk about a life-changing transformation!

From Pain to Pleasure

Isn't it fascinating that your brain can and will keep you away from pain that's completely imagined just as easily as it keeps you from pain that is actual and real?

Let's take the common experience of social anxiety. According to the National Institute of Mental Health, roughly 40 million Americans suffer from some type of social anxiety: the feeling of discomfort or fear in social interactions. It commonly involves a fear of being judged or of embarrassment, criticism, or rejection. As a result, the person feels insecure or not good enough, or assumes that others will reject them.

To give you context, *developmental social anxiety* occurs in early childhood as a normal part of growing up: it is a stage that most children grow out of. However, if it persists or resurfaces later in life, it is called *chronic social anxiety*. This comes in many forms and can vary in how it is experienced and in which type of situations.

The difference between social anxiety and the normal feeling of nervousness that most of us feel when meeting new people is that social anxiety involves an intense feeling of fear in social settings, especially ones that are unfamiliar or in which the person feels they will be judged by others.

Hundreds of famous people throughout history and in modern times have either been purported to suffer from social anxiety or have reported it themselves. The list of famously shy authors includes Harper Lee, author of *To Kill a Mockingbird*; Agatha Christie, perhaps the most famous mystery author of all time; C. S. Lewis, author of The Chronicles of Narnia; Margaret Mitchell, author of Gone with the Wind; Emily Dickinson; George Bernard Shaw; science fiction author Isaac Asimov; and

MANY CELEBRITIES SUFFER FROM SOCIAL ANXIETY.

J.K. Rowling, author of the Harry Potter series; among many others. Celebrities who have spoken of their shyness or social anxiety include movie stars like Johnny Depp, Emma Stone, and Anthony Hopkins, and singers such as Barbra Streisand, Adele, Carly Simon, Lady Gaga, and Donny Osmond.

Perhaps the most famously shy person of all time was Abraham Lincoln, who frequently spoke and wrote about his nervousness and self-consciousness about everything from his looks to his height to his country upbringing to what he felt was his lack of education. For his 1860 campaign biography, when he was asked to describe his education, Lincoln wrote one word: "Deficient."

Even after the epic debates of his Senate campaign thrust him to national fame, Lincoln was so modest that in 1859 he wrote, "I do not think myself fit for the presidency." It seems clear that he was not practicing false modesty but suffered from a form of social anxiety that lasted his entire life. How even more amazing, then, that he overcame these intense feelings of inadequacy to become one of the greatest leaders in all of history.

If all of these famous and highly successful people have suffered from some form of social anxiety, how did they overcome their fears and become so successful? And what can we learn from them to increase our own level of self-confidence?

What Are You Going to Do with Your Fear?

The answer comes back to the habit loop. Let me give you an example. In addition to all those famous people I just listed who have suffered from social anxiety, you can add one more person to the list: me.

When I was growing up, I went through the awkward stage that many teenagers go through. In my case, however, it was particularly extreme. If you were to have called central casting and asked for a nerd, you would have gotten me. My eyesight was so bad that I had to wear Coke-bottle glasses. I had a bad case of acne that covered my entire face. I didn't have shoulder-length hair; I had shoulder-*width* hair.

I had big gaps in my teeth that made me self-conscious about my smile. I was so scrawny and skinny that I looked like the definition of the 98-pound weakling. As you can imagine, when I looked in the mirror, I wasn't exactly thrilled with what I saw.

It didn't help that, like I mentioned earlier, I was driven to get straight A's. So not only did I feel unbelievably awkward because of my looks, I didn't fit in because I rarely socialized with my classmates.

I had very few friends all the way through grammar school. Then my parents and teachers decided that I should skip eighth grade and go right to high school. Since I grew up in a small town, I had gone to school with the same group of classmates from the age of kindergarten all through grammar school. When I skipped eighth grade, I had to leave behind all of my classmates that I had known and grown up with my entire life and enter a brand-new class where I didn't know anyone. So I became even shyer and quieter, if that's possible.

However—and this is something that celebrities who suffer from social anxiety seem to have in common—one way I dealt with my shyness was to appear in plays in high school. I think it had to do with wanting to be someone else. I can certainly tell you that when I was in high school, I wanted to be anyone but myself!

In any event, my social awkwardness and shyness did not translate into shyness on stage or in front of groups of people. You might wonder how that's possible. In fact, I know exactly why it happened.

THIS IS WHY I'M AN EXTROVERTED INTROVERT.

When I was very young, my father was the marketing director of a small community theater in Kennebunkport, Maine. From the time I was three years old, my brother and I would get onstage during breaks in rehearsal and perform Bert and Ernie routines from the TV show *Sesame Street* from memory.

The adults, of course, thought we were adorable, and as a result, I would get lots of attention—which is, of course, what every kid wants. As a result, from the time I was very young, I associated being onstage and performing in front of an audience with pleasure. That's why, even though I was painfully shy and awkward around people offstage, my brain created a habit loop that craved the feeling of performing onstage.

While I can't speak for celebrities like Johnny Depp or Donny Osmond, my hunch is that if you were to ask them, they probably had a similar experience growing up. In fact, when you read biographies or watch interviews of famous people, in almost every case, they talk about a single moment in their lives when they first appeared on stage in front of an audience. Maybe it was their school play or talent show. Maybe it was like my case: they came from a family of performers, and it was just part of growing up.

In any case, I believe that this childhood experience of gaining pleasure from being in front of an audience, and the subsequent craving that developed as a result, causes many performers to overcome their social anxiety in order to fulfill that craving for love and attention.

If I Can Do It, So Can You

What does this mean for you? First, social anxiety can indeed be overcome. Second, even famous people can have social anxiety. Third, you can retrain your brain to your advantage, when you understand and follow the Power Habits System.

In fact, I have discovered that anyone can develop these habits and put the right elements in place, no matter how shy or not self-confident you may feel right now. Furthermore, these habits will positively affect every area of your life, from your personal and business relationships to your health and finances.

In short, if someone like me, who had no self-confidence, can transform themselves into a person with unstoppable self-confidence, then anyone can!

In our next chapter, I'll give you the missing piece to unstoppable self-confidence. It can transform your life and help you reach your goals twice as fast with half the effort—and it takes less than five minutes a day. See you there!

4

AFFORMATIONS:
The Missing Piece
to Unstoppable
Self-Confidence

Every sentence I utter must be understood,
not as an affirmation, but as a question.

—NIELS BOHR

'd like you to consider, for a moment, your brain.
Right now, you are reading these words that I have
written. In a fraction of a second, they are being
processed by your brain, and ultimately you not only
understand what I'm saying, you are reaching your
own conclusions and forming your own opinions about
everything I say. All this happens hundreds of times
faster than I can describe it. You do all of this in the
blink of an eye, without even giving it a second thought.

Yet, if we were to look at your brain in isolation, we'd find that it weighs about 3 pounds. That's around 2 percent of the total average body weight. But did you know that 25 percent of the oxygen that's used by your body is used by your brain? Furthermore, your brain uses fully 70 percent of the glucose that your body processes when you eat food, and 25 percent of the body's nutrients are consumed by the brain. Approximately 1.5 pints of blood are pumped through your brain every 60 seconds—and if all of the blood vessels, capillaries, and other transport systems in your brain were laid end to end, they would stretch over 100,000 miles—nearly halfway to the moon!

I have often sat in awe of the miracle of the brain and of thought itself, especially when you realize that the human brain created science, religion, philosophy, mathematics, history, and every work of art that has ever existed.

If this miraculous organ, the human brain, is so incredibly powerful, how come we so often get in our own way?

The Most Powerful Tool You've Got

I'd like you to think about your brain for a moment as a tool. Right now, you are in possession of the most powerful tool on planet earth—and it's located right between your ears.

Like any tool, your brain can be used correctly or it can be misused or abused. Take a hammer, for example. Using it correctly, you can build a house, a boat, a log cabin, a desk, a chair, and thousands of other useful things. However, you can also misuse a hammer, accidentally whack your thumb with it, and cause a lot of pain!

Most people are unknowingly misusing the most powerful tool in the world, or actually using it against themselves! Why? Because very few of us were ever taught how to use our brains correctly.

> **WE GET NO TRAINING ON THE MOST IMPORTANT TOOL WE'LL EVER HAVE.**

To illustrate what I'm talking about, let me tell you a story that I have often shared in my books and training programs and with my coaching clients, called "The Shower That Changed Everything."

The Shower That Changed Everything

Did you ever notice how the best ideas seem to come to you in the shower? You're in the shower, going through your normal routine, when you suddenly have a flash of insight—the solution to the problem you've been facing or the answer to the question you've been asking. Often, it was right in front of you all along.

If you've read any of my other books like *AFFORMATIONS* or *Power Habits*, you may have heard part of this story. But in this book, I'd like to tell you the rest.

In April 1997, I was a divorced, thirty-year-old religious studies major with less than $800 to my name. I was living in a dorm room so small that if you stood in the middle and put your arms out, you could touch the walls on both sides.

At this point, I was very depressed and frustrated, because I'd been reading self-help and personal growth books my whole life, but I was definitely not successful.

That night, as I looked around my tiny dorm room, which held everything I owned in the world, I noticed something: the walls were covered with pieces of paper on which I'd written dozens of positive statements, such as *I am happy, I am wealthy, I am prosperous,* and *I am good enough.*

That night, I admitted something that I'd never wanted to admit before: that even though I'd spent most of my life trying to believe these positive statements, I never really did. In fact, the harder I tried to believe those positive things about myself, the more the cold, hard facts stared back at me and seemed to say, "Yeah, right!" So I turned out the light and went to bed feeling even more depressed.

The next day, I woke up and got in the shower, just like any other morning. Except on this particular morning, my mind was still racing from the night before. Questions were rattling in my head like:

If I've been saying these positive statements to myself for so long, how come I still don't believe them? And if I don't believe these positive statements after repeating them over and over for so many years, what's it going to take for me to finally believe something good about myself?

There's got to be something missing. But what is it?

Searching for Answers to Questions

That's when I realized that what I was doing at that very moment was asking and searching for answers to questions. I realized that *human thought itself is the process of asking and searching for answers to questions.*

Suddenly, a question formed in my mind—a simple question that changed everything:

If human thought is the process of asking and searching for answers to questions, *why are we going around making* statements *we don't believe?*

Suddenly, I understood why I never believed all those positive statements I'd been repeating over and over all those years. It all came down to one simple thing. Of course!

I realized that it doesn't matter how long or how often we repeat these positive statements to ourselves; if we don't fix this one thing, all of our hard work will be for naught.

Something else occurred to me. I realized that there were millions of people just like me—people who are trying hard to change their lives, people who are following the rules that we were given, but who still haven't manifested the lifestyle they want—because they didn't believe the positive statements they'd been saying to themselves either.

At that moment, I realized that if we were to start to *ask ourselves the right questions* and *stop asking the wrong questions,* it would change everything.

And for the first time, I knew what I was put here on earth to do.

The Rest of the Story

If you've heard me tell that story before, you know that I launched my company, SuccessClinic.com, and that people from around the world have used my AFFORMATIONS Method to make more money, lose hundreds of pounds, find their soulmates, save their marriages, and profoundly transform their lives.

Yet there's even more to the story. After my epiphany, I jumped out of the shower, ran back to my dorm room, sat down at my Apple computer and wrote down everything I had just thought of.

As I stared at the words glowing on my computer screen, I thought: *If I accept the truth of these new questions—and start acting as if they were true—then my life would have to change.*

Then I wrote another question, then another, and another. I kept writing and writing as fast as I could. For the first time in my life, everything finally made sense.

This is so cool! I thought. *I can't believe no one's ever thought of this before!* Then I had another thought, one that stopped me in my tracks: *What am I supposed to do now?*

I didn't yet have an answer to that question. That's why, even though I knew my life was about to change, I still didn't know how to change it. I went about the business of being a broke thirty-year-old religious studies major—and tucked my discovery away until I could figure out what to do with it.

Six months later, on October 20, 1997, I had the second epiphany that changed my life. I realized the existence of a condition I named *success anorexia,* which causes people to hold themselves back from the level of success they're capable of. That discovery led to the publication of my first book, *Permission to Succeed,* and eventually to my other books, seminars, speeches, and one-on-one and group coaching programs.

And my clients kept getting amazing, life-changing results like:

- Getting promotions after feeling completely stuck in their careers
- Adding six, seven, and eight figures to their income without stress
- Losing weight after they'd tried every diet and exercise program on the market
- Finding the man or woman of their dreams after giving up on relationships
- Starting the business they'd been dreaming of
- Writing books that had been left unfinished for years
- Quitting smoking after they'd tried everything else
- Winning golf tournaments and other sporting events for the first time

And thousands more stories like this.

Then those clients began to tell their friends, and those friends told *their* friends ... and so on and so on . . . and that's how the AFFORMATIONS revolution was born.

And it all started with a simple question that I asked in the shower more than twenty-six years ago.

What Is a Question?

A *question* is defined as an expression of inquiry that calls for a reply. When you ask a question, what happens?

For example, right now, you're probably thinking, *I don't know—what happens when I ask a question?*

Do you see that? When you ask a question, *your mind automatically begins to search for an answer.*

You can't help it. It's automatic. It happens without your volition. Searching for an answer to a question is perhaps the most basic function of the human mind.

On that fateful morning of the Shower That Changed Everything, I realized that this simple truth of human consciousness may hold the answer to solving life's biggest problems. Here's what I mean.

How You Create Your Life

On that fateful morning in April 1997, I realized that you create your life in two ways: by the statements you make to yourself and others and by the questions you ask yourselves and others.

Traditional success teachers have focused a great deal of time and energy on telling you to change your statements. For millions of people, that old method worked—but for millions of people, it didn't.

However, until the Shower That Changed Everything, no one had fully shown how to harness the awesome power of what happens when you *change your internal and external questions*.

Here's a fun exercise I like to do with my clients and in my keynote speeches. Let's take a classic positive affirmation: *"I am rich."*

Try it; say it with me now: *"I am rich."*

What's your brain saying right now? *"Yeah, right!"*

We *want* to believe this positive statement, yet most of us just don't.

THIS IS WHY AFFIRMATIONS TEND NOT TO WORK VERY WELL.

When I discovered my AFFORMATIONS Method, I asked, "If we don't believe the statement, what would the *question* be?"

Take the statement *"I am rich"*—to which your brain replies, *"Yeah, right."*

What would the question be?

"Why am I so rich?"

Go ahead and ask yourself, *"Why am I so rich?"* What's happening right now? Your brain is searching for the answer!

The Law of Sowing and Reaping

We all know about the law of sowing and reaping: *As you sow, so shall you reap.* What are we sowing? We're sowing seeds of thought.

Yet what are most people doing? Sowing lousy thought seeds!

They're unconsciously asking themselves questions like: *"Why am I so broke? Why am I so fat? Why can't I lose weight? Why can't I get more clients? Why is there more month left at the end of the money?"*

Ask lousy questions and what do you get? Lousy answers! And that creates a lousy life!

What if we were to flip the whole thing on its head and start asking empowering QUESTIONS that lead to phenomenal ANSWERS and would FORM a wonderful LIFE?

As I was standing there in the shower on April 24, 1997, I said: *"Holy cow, I think I just invented something!"* So I had to give it a name. And the name that I gave it was AFFORMATIONS.

How I Named My AFFORMATIONS Method

I invented the word *Afformation* because it's perfectly legitimate to invent a new word to describe a new technology or a new way of looking at the universe. For example, words like *Google, software,* and *Internet,* are new terms because these technologies have only been around for a short time. They were invented to describe new technologies. Of course, now we use these words every day. Well, my discovery of AFFORMATIONS is *a new technology of the mind.*

The word *affirmation* comes from the Latin word *firmare,* which means *to make firm.* The word *afformation* comes from the Latin *formare,* which means *to form* or *give shape to.* I often ask my coaching clients, "What if you're making something *firm,* but it's in the *wrong form?* That would be forming a life you *didn't* want!"

AFFORMATIONS ARE A NEW TECHNOLOGY OF THE MIND.

Now, for the first time in history, using my AFFORMATIONS Method, you can take conscious control of the questions you're asking. Change the questions, change your habits, and change your life!

How to Use AFFORMATIONS

I've taught my AFFORMATIONS Method to countless groups around the world, from business owners in Australia to working moms in New York, from direct sales professionals in Dallas to multimillionaire CEOs in Florida. In countless thousands of cases, these four simple steps have changed people's lives for the better.

Step One: Ask Yourself What You Want

If you were in New York City and wanted to take a road trip to meet a friend in Los Angeles, which approach would you choose?

Option 1. Pick a specific location, date, and time for your meeting, figure out the fastest route to take, and then start on your journey—giving yourself enough time to allow for the inevitable delays, detours, and roadblocks.

Option 2. Jump in your car and drive west until you hit the ocean, drive up and down the coast until you find the city of Los Angeles, and then ask everyone you meet to tell you where your friend is.

You'd pick the first option, right? It's far more efficient and produces a nearly guaranteed result of meeting up with your friend.

Why, then, do most people choose the second approach when pursuing their dreams and living their lives? Armed with only a vague idea of what they want and how to get there, they wander through life, hoping against hope that they will reach their destination.

This approach doesn't work for success any better than it works for a cross-country trip. Setting goals gives you a clear destination, the focus to keep you on track, and the awareness to guide your choices and actions.

That's why the first step of the AFFORMATIONS Method is to *ask yourself what you really want.* You can use goals you've already written, or you can start from scratch. It's completely up to you.

If this were a traditional success program, the next thing I would tell you is that after you've set your goals, you should make a plan to get there. Sounds logical, doesn't it? Just as with our cross-country trip, once you know your destination, you'd just pack up your stuff and head out, right?

That approach *would* work if not for one tiny little detail: that annoying but inescapable fact that most people don't believe they can reach their goals in the first place.

Step Two: Form a Question That Assumes That What You Want Is Already True

This is the key to creating AFFORMATIONS that will change your life!

Let me give you an example. I was in Virginia leading a private workshop when a young couple came up to me jumping up and down with excitement. They said they'd heard me teach AFFORMATIONS at the national convention for one of the world's largest direct sales companies. Here's what they told me:

Our dream was to qualify for the car our company offers as an incentive for sales performance. Since that was our goal, we'd been using affirmations for the past four years just as we'd been told: we made audios and listened to them over and over, repeated them all the time to each other, and placed them all over our refrigerator.

We even hung affirmation signs in the shower to try to reach our goal . . . but all we got was a bunch of wet words!

After hearing you speak about AFFORMATIONS during your keynote speech at our national convention, we were very excited. We realized that AFFORMATIONS really *are* the missing piece to having abundance, because they allowed us to bridge the gap between the positive statements we were saying and our own inner beliefs.

We started asking each other our new, empowering questions, placed them all over our refrigerator, and talked about our new AFFORMATIONS day after day.

The results were absolutely amazing! We heard you speak at our national convention in July. By August, we realized we were doing a lot of things differently because of the AFFORMATIONS we were using. And in September, our production had increased so much that we finally qualified for our first company car!

In short, after *four years* of not reaching our goal using the traditional method, *we got the exact results we wanted in less than 12 weeks thanks to your methods*. Thank you, Noah!

Step Three: Accept the Truth of Your New Questions

When I tell my coaching clients to accept the truth of their new questions, they often ask me what that means. There are four essential ways you can accept the truth of your new empowering AFFORMATIONS. You can:

1. Read them.
2. Write them.

3. Say them.
4. Listen to them.

These are the four modes of human communication. *Accepting the truth of your new questions* means using all of these modes as often as possible.

While all four modes are essential, my experience has shown that the one that produces the fastest results is listening. Why?

Most of us could hardly count the number of negative thoughts we've had about ourselves. When you think these negative thoughts, you're effectively listening to them in your head. In my books and coaching programs, I call this your *negative reflection.*

When you listen to empowering AFFORMATIONS, you will begin to drown out that negative voice and stop giving power to it. That's also why I invented iAfform® Audios. iAfform Audios are empowering AFFORMATIONS set to inspiring music that you can listen to anytime, anywhere. You can listen to your iAfform Audios while you're eating, exercising, working, or playing, in the car, at home, or in your office. Many of my clients even listen to their iAfform Audios while they sleep.

Because of the demand from clients around the world, I've created special iAfform Audios for many different areas of life, including:

- Ultimate Self-Confidence
- Ultimate Wealth
- Faster Weight Loss
- Deep, Blissful Sleep
- Living Your Life Purpose
- . . . and many more.

For example, Michael from Germany sent me this amazing story:

Hi Noah, I've bought every *iAfform Power Pack* you have. You might be wondering why I have gone Afformation crazy, but your AFFORMATIONS changed my life in a few minutes last June.

I used to be a chronic procrastinator. I also believed that I was unable to be, do, or have anything I wanted: money, to keep a job, and so on, and my self-confidence was nonexistent. I did not realize that until I started using your iAfform Wealth Power Pack. In one night, in just a few minutes, there were *big* changes!

When I came across your work, my wife Silvia and I had our divorce papers on the desk, waiting to be signed. Then I shared your AFFORMATIONS with her, and now we are best friends and in love again. We also have a list of 26 AFFORMATIONS that we write every morning and read every chance we get throughout the day. I also would like to get certified as one of your coaches, and I hope it's soon. Thank you, Noah, for changing our lives!

I encourage you to try iAfform Audios by downloading my free 60-Second iAfform Stress Buster at **iAfform.com** (yes, using my AFFORMATIONS Method, you can bust your stress in 60 seconds or less!).

Which brings us to the fourth step of the method—the one you absolutely must take to manifest the results you want.

Step Four: Take Action Based on Your New Assumptions

My AFFORMATIONS Method is based on science, not magic. For example, you cannot simply Afform: *Why am I so healthy?*, then continue to eat junk food, not exercise, and expect to drop the pounds!

Similarly, you can't simply Afform, *Why am I so confident?* then never do anything *different* than what you've done in the past, and expect to grow your self-confidence—any more than you would expect a plant to grow if it were never watered or nourished.

The point of AFFORMATIONS is not to try to trick your mind but to use it properly. That's why following this method will help you to dramatically increase your self-confidence and reach your goals twice as fast with half the effort.

If Nothing Changes, Nothing Changes

Although AFFORMATIONS are the fastest and most effective belief-change method ever invented, you have to do still more if you want to see life-changing results. Just keep taking action and getting the support and guidance you need from a trusted coach or mentor.

For example, learn more about our one-on-one and group coaching programs like the Inner Game Breakthrough at **BreakthroughwithNoah.com**. You can also get my AFFORMATIONS Advantage program at **Afformations.com** and my *Book of AFFORMATIONS*, published by Hay House, at **AfformationsBook.com**.

In the next chapter, I'll show you how to master your Inner and Outer Games of self-confidence and give you some simple but highly effective exercises to help you master the Power Habits of Unstoppable Self-Confidence. Let's go!

5

Mastering the Inner Game of Self-Confidence

It took me a long time not to judge myself through someone else's eyes.

—SALLY FIELD

On January 8, 1935, in a tiny two-room house in Tupelo, Mississippi, a teenager named Gladys gave birth to her first child, a boy. The boy's identical twin brother had been delivered stillborn thirty-five minutes before him. Growing up as an only child, the boy formed an especially close bond with his mother.

While Gladys raised the boy, her husband, Vernon, moved from one odd job to the next. The family often relied on help from neighbors and government food assistance. In 1938, they lost their home after Vernon was found guilty of altering a check. He was jailed for eight months, and Gladys and their son moved in with relatives.

In September 1941, the boy entered first grade at East Tupelo Consolidated, where his instructors regarded him as "average." He was encouraged to enter a singing contest after impressing his schoolteacher with a rendition of "Old Shep" during morning prayers.

The contest, held at the Mississippi-Alabama Fair and Dairy Show on October 3, 1945, was the boy's first public performance: dressed as a cowboy, he stood on a chair to reach the microphone and sang "Old Shep." He placed fifth.

A few months later, for his eleventh birthday, the boy received his first guitar; he had been hoping for either a bicycle or a rifle. He would later recall, "I took the guitar, and I watched people, and I learned to play a little bit. But I would never sing in public. I was very shy about it."

Entering a new school for sixth grade in September 1946, the boy was regarded as a loner. The following year, he began bringing his guitar to school daily. He played and sang during lunchtime, but he was often teased as a trashy kid who played hillbilly music.

By then, the family was living in a largely African-American neighborhood. The boy, a fan of Mississippi Slim's show on the Tupelo radio station WELO, was described as "crazy about music" by Slim's younger brother, who began teaching him chords on the guitar. When the boy was twelve years old, Slim scheduled him for two on-air performances. Even though the boy was overcome by stage fright the first time, he succeeded in performing the following week.

In November 1948, the family moved to Memphis, Tennessee, where they lived in public rooming houses. In eighth grade, the boy got a C in music because his teacher told him he had no aptitude for singing.

Too shy to perform openly, the boy was often bullied by classmates who viewed him as a mama's boy. In 1950, a neighbor named Jesse Lee Denson began tutoring the boy on the guitar, and finally he overcame his shyness enough to perform in the Annual Minstrel show in April 1953.

He later said that that performance did much for his reputation. He said: "I wasn't popular in school . . . I failed music—the only thing I ever failed. And then they entered me in this talent show . . . when I came onstage I heard people kind of rumbling and whispering and so forth, 'cause nobody knew I even sang. It was amazing how popular I became after that."

In August 1953, the boy—now a young man— walked into the offices of Sun Records, owned by a man named Sam Phillips. The young man aimed to pay for a few minutes of studio time to record a two-sided disk as a gift for his mother.

He then failed an audition for a local vocal quartet, the Songfellows, because, he later said, "They told me I couldn't sing." He was by then working as a truck driver. A friend suggested he contact the leader of a local professional band, but he was rejected after a tryout. The band leader even advised the young man to stick to truck driving "because you're never going to make it as a singer."

Then, on July 5, 1954, the young man was back at Sun Records to cut another record, but the recording session wasn't going well. The young man and the musicians were just about to pack up and go home when he took out his guitar and launched into a 1946 blues number, Arthur Crudup's "That's All Right."

One of the musicians later recalled, "All of a sudden, he just started singing this song, jumping around and acting the fool, and then the bass player picked up his bass, and he started acting the fool, too; and then I started playing along.

"Sam Phillips then stuck his head out of the control booth and said, 'What are you guys doing?' And we said, 'We don't know.' 'Well, back up,' he said, 'try to find a place to start, and do it again.'"

Phillips quickly began taping the session; three days later, popular Memphis DJ Dewey Phillips played the young man's recording of "That's All Right" on his *Red, Hot, and Blue* show. The phones rang off the hook with people demanding to find out who the singer was.

That's the story of how Elvis Presley went on to become the world's first superstar, one of the most important cultural icons of the twentieth century and the "King of Rock and Roll."

The Inner Game of Self-Confidence

You might think this story is about how Elvis Presley overcame a hardscrabble childhood, being told he wasn't talented, and incredible odds to become the most famous superstar of the twentieth century. And you'd be right.

However, we all know how Elvis's story ended at the tender age of forty-two after years of abusing his body with overeating and drugs.

What is sad about Elvis's story is that for generations to come, it will be told, not as one of the greatest examples of how to overcome overwhelming odds to become successful, but as a cautionary tale of what can happen when a person can't handle success. That's what I want to talk with you about in this chapter.

What do I mean by *Inner Game* and *Outer Game*? What's the difference, and why is it so important to master both of these if you want to have unstoppable self-confidence?

Let's start with your Inner Game, which consists of the things that happen between your ears. You cannot see them directly, although you can see the effects everywhere. Your Inner Game consists of things like your thoughts, beliefs, desires, priorities, values, and character. These all take place inside of you. Your Inner Game is who you are and what you think and believe about yourself.

By contrast, your Outer Game consists of the things you can see directly and that affect your results in life: your behaviors and habits, your lifestyle and actions, your systems and strategies. Your Outer Game consists of the things you do and the actions that express your personality.

Why, then, is it so important to master both your Inner and your Outer Games if you want to have unstoppable self-confidence and success?

THIS IS THE DIFFERENCE BETWEEN THE INNER GAME AND THE OUTER GAME.

Elvis Presley had mastered the Outer Game in every way imaginable. He was rich and famous—probably the most famous person in the world at the time of his death. He dated many of the world's most beautiful women, met with presidents, and had hundreds of millions of adoring fans around the world. From the outside, it certainly looked as though Elvis had everything that a person could possibly want in terms of material success.

If that's true, how could Elvis have effectively cut his life so short? *Because he had not mastered his Inner Game.*

Someone who masters their Inner Game would not abuse drugs, because they would realize what an incredible toll drugs take on the human body; using them constitutes a form of self-abuse. We also know about Elvis's manager, "Colonel" Tom Parker (not an actual colonel at all), controlling nearly every aspect of Elvis's life and career, taking up to 50 percent of the earnings from Elvis's movies and recordings. Priscilla Presley, Elvis's widow, has been quoted as saying that "Elvis detested the business side of his career. He would sign a contract without even reading it."

Someone who masters their Inner Game would not allow someone else to abuse or manipulate them. Nor would they sign a contract without reading it.

Can you see how Elvis's life reveals that while he had unquestionably mastered the Outer Game of success, he never mastered his Inner Game? I believe that was why his life was cut far too short.

Just Because You're Rich and Famous . . .

I'm sure you can think of dozens of other examples like Elvis Presley—celebrities who had seemingly mastered the Outer Game but who nevertheless died young, because they did not master their Inner Game. For example: Marilyn Monroe, Andy Gibb, Chris Farley, River Phoenix, John Belushi, Heath Ledger, Kurt Cobain, Jimi Hendrix, Amy Winehouse, Jim Morrison, and so many more. Sadly, the list goes on and on.

Just because you're rich and famous does not mean that you have everything figured out; nor does it mean that you've mastered your Inner Game. The actor and comedian Jim Carrey once said, "I actually wish that everyone could become rich and famous, so that they would find out it's not the answer."

Your Perception of Value

Remember, your Inner Game consists of the things that happen between your ears. They are invisible to the outside world but affect everything you think, say, and do in every situation.

The Inner Game essentially has to do with your *perception of value*: specifically, your perception of your own value to yourself, to other people, and to the world.

Let me tell you a story to illustrate this concept. When I was twenty-five years old, I was at a very low point in my life. I had been forced to retire from my career as a professional ballet dancer because of a career-ending injury. I ended up with no money, no job, no connections, very little education, and no idea what to do with the rest of my life.

I found myself in Los Angeles looking for work. After a series of dead-end jobs, I became very depressed. I was living in a small apartment with no friends and very little money. After applying for what I thought was my dream job and being rejected yet again, I decided to take my own life.

Problem: I didn't own a gun. I thought of how I could kill myself without a gun. I remembered hearing how the exhaust from your car engine would kill you if you kept your car running in a closed garage. I decided to do it that way.

Problem: I didn't have a garage either. In the apartment building where I lived, there were only open auto bays, and there was no way to asphyxiate myself in the open air.

I decided to get in my car and drive around the neighborhood until I found an unlocked garage that I could pull my car in, shut the door behind me, and kill myself.

About fifteen minutes later, I found myself parked on a strange street in front of a garage with its door wide open. I could drive right in, shut the door behind me, close my eyes . . . and that would be that.

Throughout all of this, I was perfectly calm. I wasn't mad. I wasn't hysterical. I wasn't even upset. I remember the moment that I decided to take my own life as a crystalline moment of clarity. It was as if a switch had flipped in my mind: I accepted that I was going to do it, and that was that—as simple a decision as going to the grocery store.

But now, staring at the reality of what I was about to do, I paused. *Think about what you're doing,* someone or something seemed to say inside of me. *Are you sure you want to do this?*

And then I saw it: the thing that saved my life.

Parked in the corner of the garage was a child's bicycle. It had a white seat and those white things you hold on to at the ends of the handlebars. It looked just like a bike that I'd had when I was a kid.

THAT'S WHEN I SAW THE THING THAT SAVED MY LIFE.

And I thought, *Wait a minute. This isn't an abandoned*

home. A family must live here. What are they going to do when they come home and find my dead body in their garage?

In my mind's eye, I saw a woman coming home and screaming in shock and terror. I saw a man trying to console the woman, but her being inconsolable, crying hysterically. I saw the bicycle's owner, a child, standing there, not understanding what was happening but knowing something was terribly wrong. And I saw my horribly selfish act traumatizing this family (whom I did not know) for the rest of their lives.

I realized that I couldn't do this to them. Even though I didn't know who they were, and will never know, I recognized that what I was about to do wasn't fair to them.

I turned my car around and drove home. And that was the last time I ever considered killing myself.

I share that story with you to show you that your actions spring from *your perception of your own value.*

When I made the decision to commit suicide, it was based on my perception that my life had no value, and that I and the rest of the world would be better off if I were dead.

It's clear that when someone holds the perception that their life has no value, they are going to act as if that perception were true—because *perception is reality to the perceiver.*

Perception Is Reality to the Perceiver

When you believe something to be true, you are going to act as if it were true, whether it is or not. For example, for centuries, humans believed that the earth was the center of the universe and that the sun goes around the earth. Our outer senses showed us that this belief was true. Just walk outside and you could see: "Of course the sun goes around the earth! What's wrong with you, dummy? Anyone can see that!"

It wasn't until a fellow named Copernicus came along and published a book that said, "Uh, guys— guess what? The earth is going around the sun!"

Copernicus was clever enough not to have this book published until he was dead. Otherwise, who knows what would have happened to him? Because even when presented with scientific facts, many people find it hard to change their beliefs.

When you believe something, you will behave as if that belief is true, even if it isn't. Because I believed that my life had no value and that the people in my life would be happier if I weren't around, I behaved that way—and nearly took my own life as a result.

To change your behavior, you first have to change your beliefs—specifically, your beliefs about your own value to yourself, to other people, and to the world. In fact, I am convinced that the principal reason people suffer from low self-confidence is that they don't understand their own value.

WHEN YOU BELIEVE SOMETHING, YOU'LL BEHAVE TO MAKE IT TRUE.

How Do You Treat Someone You Value?

Let me show you what I mean by asking you to do this simple exercise with me. I'd like you to think about someone that you truly value. Maybe it's your spouse, your best friend, or your children. When you think of them, how do you feel? You want only the best for them, right? You don't want anything bad to happen to them. You would be devastated if you lost them. You would go to any length to protect and take care of them.

That's what value is. That is what the perception of value represents. It means that you don't want any harm to come to this person, and if you ever lost that person, there would be a great loss in your life.

Well, that feeling you have about someone else is how I want you to start perceiving *yourself.* For instance, do you realize how valuable you are? Do you truly *get* your own value to others and to the world?

For most of us, the answer to these questions is no.

That's one of the main reasons that so many people have low self-confidence. It's also why in order to build unstoppable self-confidence, you need to have a proper understanding of your own value.

IS THIS HOW YOU'D TREAT SOMEONE YOU VALUE?

Now here's where things really get interesting.

Where Does Your Value Come From?

I'd like you to think about this for a moment: where do we humans get our perception of our worth or value? The answer often depends on whether you are male or female. Think about it. Since the beginning of human history, female human beings have been told that their worth comes from their physical bodies.

Since the beginning of human history, female human beings have been told, both implicitly and explicitly, that their worth is primarily based on their *physical bodies*. This perception is entirely wrong. It is *not* true that a woman's worth comes from her physical body. But that doesn't stop millions of people from believing it to be true, simply because that is

Doesn't it make sense, then, that your perception of your worth is going to depend greatly on whether you believe it comes from your *physical body* or your *material body?*

This is where most people get their perception of value.

Going back to my earlier example, I was so depressed and had no self-confidence largely because I was broke and had no money. And I had no money because no one had ever taught me how to make money or even shown me how life really works. I became depressed and suicidal mainly because I felt like a material failure: I had no idea how to create material success. Most men in my position would have probably felt the same way I did. I made the decision to take my own life largely because of *my perception of my inability to succeed.*

For today's women, it's even harder: not only are women expected to look perfect, they're also expected to make as much money as their male counterparts. Today's woman, in addition to being told that her worth comes from her *physical* body, is being told that her worth comes from her *material* body as well! She is essentially being told that she has to not only look perfect but also make money and provide for her family—the traditional material pressure that for

what women have been told since the beg
human history.

If you look around, you see this per
reinforced everywhere—on magazine covers th
women as physical objects, in TV commercial
constantly tell women that they need to lose weig
order to be happy, and so on. Can you see how
erroneous belief would affect a woman?

Now let's look at the other sex: men. Where ha
they been told their worth comes from? Again, sinc
the beginning of human history, men have been told
that their worth comes from their possessions, their
title, job, net worth, holdings, the size of their bank
account—what I call their *material bodies* (as opposed
to their *physical bodies*).

This perception about men is, again, completely
wrong. It is *not* true that a man's worth comes from
his material body. But the fact that it's not true doesn't
stop millions of people from believing it to be true,
simply because, again, that is what men have been
told since the beginning of human history.

And can you see how this erroneous belief would
affect a male? Just look around, and you'll see this
perception reinforced everywhere—in magazines that
tell men they need to be more successful and make
more money, on TV shows that show money as the
be-all and end-all of the universe, and so on.

most of human history was relegated to the male of the household.

How This Is Affecting You Right Now

Let's look at how these different perceptions show up in our everyday lives. Let's say you are a man on your way to work in the morning. What thoughts are going through your head? I believe that most men's thoughts revolve around things like money, providing for their families, the deals they're going to do that day, getting a promotion at work, paying for their kids' college tuition, setting aside enough money for retirement, and the like.

As we've seen, our behaviors are caused by our beliefs. Let's say that you're on your way to work, and as you're thinking about these things, you're feeling pretty good. You like your job, you feel in control of most situations that come up, you're making good money, you like the people you work with, and you're able to provide for your family. I'm sure you've met people like this, and hopefully you're one of them!

If these are your thoughts and beliefs on your way to work, what are your actions going to be? They would almost certainly be things like smiling, thinking good thoughts, picturing how well the day is going to go, or maybe even whistling or singing on the way into work.

What if the opposite is true? What if you're not happy on the way to work? What if a whole different set of thoughts is going through your head? What if you don't like your job or even hate it? What if you don't feel in control or don't feel you have any say in what happens at your job? What if you don't like the people you work with? What if you're not making enough money for retirement? What if you're afraid that you won't be able to provide for your family?

Again, if these are your thoughts on the way to work, your actions are going to reflect those beliefs. You'll probably be grouchy and unhappy. Instead of picturing how well things will go, you'll think of all the awful things that are going to happen, and you will certainly not be smiling, whistling, or singing.

For most of my life, I held the opinion that nothing I did would ever be good enough. Because I honestly believed that, it seemed true to me. I won a National Merit Scholarship, graduated at the top of my class, got straight A's, and became a professional ballet dancer—all things that sound pretty impressive. They probably would have impressed me—if someone else had done them! But because *I* had done them, I was entirely unimpressed by my own achievements. My own low

How can you achieve metaphysical attractiveness? First, by understanding your own value. Second, by understanding the other person's value by remembering how incorrectly society judges both men and women. Third, by consistently reminding yourself and reminding others of their true value apart from their looks or material success.

See the truth of the person you're talking to; see that they have hopes, fears, dreams, goals, and desires just like you; and see beyond the mask that most of us put on every day to hide those same hopes, fears, dreams, goals, and desires from everyone else.

Achieving Inner Game mastery comes down to seeing beyond the labels to the truth of every person you meet—and to remind yourself of who you really are, every day of your life.

In our next chapter, I'll show you how to transform shyness into unstoppable self-confidence by looking at specific examples in your business, your work, and your home life. I'll also show you how to transform shyness into unstoppable self-confidence in just three simple steps. Let's go!

opinion of myself clouded my judgment and caus[
my utter lack of self-confidence.

Achieving Inner Game Mastery

As we all know, people treat a woman a certain way if
she is physically attractive and treat a man a certain
way if he is rich. We all know this, yet we rarely talk
about it. That's why part of this work is to get it out in
the open, so you can achieve Inner Game mastery and
stop following the crazy rules that society lays down
for us. An attractive woman may be insecure about
the fact that some day, her looks will be gone. And that
uber-successful man? He's likely to be insecure about
the fact people are only nice to him because he's rich.

That's where we reach the final level of Inner Game
mastery: to remember who you really are and to treat
others as they really are—neither better nor worse than
you or anyone else, yet all equal in the eyes of God.

There is something very attractive about someone
who knows who they are and treats everyone with
the same respect. I am not talking about physical
appearance here. I am talking about something
deeper, which I call *metaphysical attractiveness*: a
term I created to describe the quality of a person who
attracts others simply by virtue of their character and
how they treat others, as well as themselves.

6

Transforming Shyness Into Unstoppable Self-Confidence

Always be yourself–express yourself,
have faith in yourself. Do not go out and look
for a successful personality and duplicate it.

—BRUCE LEE

In early 1960, a married couple in California with four kids decided to get a divorce. Their names were Amos and Janet. Amos was an itinerant cook, and Janet worked at a hospital. The three older kids, Sandra, Larry, and Tommy, went with their father, and Jimmy, the youngest, stayed with their mother.

Amos's work required him to move around a lot, which meant that the three older kids drifted from school to school and were never able to form lasting friendships. In addition, Amos married two more times after Janet, the second marriage bringing five stepbrothers and sisters. Amos decided to leave that marriage in the middle of the night; he packed up his three kids and drove off. By the time Tommy had reached the age of ten, he had had three mothers, five grammar schools, and ten houses.

All of this moving around and uncertainty made Tommy painfully shy. He later described himself as a "Bible-toting evangelical teenager" and also as "a geek, a spaz, and horribly, painfully, terribly shy." However, he also became the guy who'd yell out funny captions during films. He was not popular with either his teachers or fellow students.

Eventually, in 1966, Amos settled in Oakland, which brought young Tommy yet another new mother and three more stepsisters. Sandra would return to her mother, leaving Tommy and Larry to live in the basement of their new home.

In Oakland, Tommy became interested in pursuits like space and baseball, and became "the loud one"—a trick he'd learned when trying to get attention in a succession of new schools. He also spent four years with a congregation of born-again Christians, leading Bible readings with the First Covenant Church. This was an attempt to fit in, find a steady family, and combat his loneliness.

Tommy also began acting in school plays and eventually studied theater in college, because, as he would say later, "acting classes looked like the best place for a guy who liked to make a lot of noise and be rather flamboyant."

During his years studying theater, Tommy met a man named Vincent Dowling, director of the Great Lakes Theater Festival in Cleveland, who offered him a job as an intern. That internship stretched into a three-year assignment covering all aspects of theater production, including lighting, set design, and stage management. Tommy decided to drop out of college and then won the 1978 Cleveland Critics Circle Award for best actor for his portrayal of Proteus in Shakespeare's *Two Gentlemen of Verona*.

In 1979, Tommy moved to New York City, where he made his film debut in the low-budget slasher film *He Knows You're Alone* and was cast as the lead role in an off-off Broadway production. One night, an agent caught his performance and ended up signing him.

The following year, Tom Hanks landed his first big role on the TV show *Bosom Buddies* and eventually went on to star in hit movies like *Splash, A League of*

Their Own, *Saving Private Ryan*, *Toy Story*, *Forrest Gump*, and many more.

Tom Hanks' movies have now grossed over $9 billion in the United States and over $15 billion worldwide, making him one of the highest-grossing actors in movie history.

He Didn't Think He Could Do It

What's fascinating about Tom Hanks' story is not just how he went from, in his own words, "horribly, painfully, terribly shy" to one of the biggest movie stars of all time. What's also remarkable is that the TV show *Bosom Buddies* ran for just two seasons, and even though the people who saw him knew that Hanks was going to be a big star, he himself didn't.

One of the coproducers of that series, Ian Praiser, said in an interview with *Rolling Stone* magazine, "The first day I saw Tom on the set, I thought, 'Too bad he won't be in television for long.' I knew he'd be a movie star in two years."

But as much as Praiser knew it, he was not able to convince Hanks. Hanks' best friend Tom Lizzio told *Rolling Stone*, "The television show had come out of nowhere. Then out of nowhere it got canceled. Tom figured he'd be back to pulling ropes and hanging lights in a theater."

How, then, can we transform shyness into unstoppable self-confidence? By first understanding what shyness is, what causes it, and then by taking simple, practical steps to overcome our own shyness and transform it into unstoppable self-confidence.

Why Overcome Shyness Anyway?

Why overcome shyness in the first place? What's wrong with being shy and quiet? Aren't there enough loudmouths in the world? We don't really need any more boisterous people, do we?

These are all valid questions and should be addressed before we move forward. So let's answer the question: why overcome shyness in the first place? And is being shy the same thing as being introverted?

In her best-selling book *Quiet: The Power of Introverts in a World That Can't Stop Talking*, author Susan Cain argues that there is a difference between shyness and introversion. She describes the difference like this: "Shyness is the fear of social disapproval or humiliation, while introversion is a preference for environments

SHYNESS IS INHERENTLY PAINFUL; INTROVERSION IS NOT.

that are not overstimulating. Shyness is inherently painful; introversion is not."

Shyness is the feeling of fear or awkwardness when a person is in social settings, particularly in new situations or with new people. As I mentioned earlier in this book, stronger forms of shyness are often called social anxiety or even social phobia.

While there are many possible causes, one of the main characteristics of shyness is that it is caused by the fear of what other people will think of you—what Napoleon Hill referred to in *Think and Grow Rich* as "the fear of criticism."

This fear of criticism, or fear of what other people will think of you, causes the individual to become scared to do what they want to do or say what they want to say, because they are too afraid of what other people will do or say. This in turn often leads the person to simply avoid social settings altogether.

Unfortunately, most of us were not taught in school or by our parents how to interact with other human beings—it was just something we were expected to somehow know!

I don't know about you, but I can't remember much of the geometry, algebra or chemistry that I learned in high school, but I sure could have used a class called "How to Get Along with People" or "How to Make Friends," and especially "How to Be Yourself In a World That Keeps Trying to Change You!"

Why I Felt More Comfortable With Books Than People

Like Tom Hanks, I was painfully, horribly shy growing up. I can think of many factors that either caused or contributed to my shyness. For one, my family moved a lot when I was growing up, because my parents rented different apartments but found that they kept not being able to afford the payments, so we would have to move again and again. As it turned out, I lived in fourteen different homes before my tenth birthday.

I was also very self-conscious about my looks, having Coke-bottle glasses, a face full of acne, and a huge mop of curly hair. I always wanted to look like the guys I saw on television, who had perfect hair, didn't wear glasses, and whose skin wasn't covered in acne.

However, what contributed the most to my shyness was that I simply didn't know what to say around other people. I always felt far more comfortable curled up in a corner of the library, reading a book, than being in a room talking with people. One running joke in my family was that if my parents ever wanted to punish me, they wouldn't send me to my room—they would send outside to play! It wasn't until after years of studying self-help and personal growth programs that I was able to overcome my shyness.

In any case, I believe that some people naturally tend to withdraw from other people in social settings. Yet in most cases, other factors also seem to be involved with shyness—for example, when someone's family moved a lot when they were growing up: a common theme I've heard among many of my clients who have reported being shy.

Is It Wrong to Be Shy?

I think the answer to that question again comes down to the difference between being shy and being introverted. I don't think there's any doubt that I would be classified as an introvert; on the other hand, I absolutely love speaking in front of an audience! In fact, I far prefer speaking to an audience of a thousand people than going to a party where I don't know anyone.

So let's further examine the distinction between shyness and introversion. Let's say you're about to enter a business meeting with an important potential client, someone who could mean a lot of business for you and your company. Let's further imagine that the outcome of this meeting could mean the difference between a big payday for you and your not getting that bonus or promotion you've been working so hard for.

Let's amp up the pressure even more by saying that along with this client, the president of your company is going to be there, because they told you to give this presentation to land this big client (or what is often referred to as a "whale").

So here you are, about to walk into this meeting with the whale and your boss, as well as other people from both sides who will be there too. *What's going through your mind right now?*

THIS IS PROBABLY WHAT'S GOING THROUGH YOUR MIND IN THAT SITUATION.

Many things will certainly be going through your mind as you're getting ready to enter this meeting. For example, you may be thinking, *"I sure hope I don't mess this up. What if I say something stupid? What if I don't land this client? What's going to happen to me if I make a mistake?"*

As you can see, these questions will not exactly help you feel confident as you walk into the room. Quite the opposite: as I showed you in the chapter on AFFORMATIONS, you are asking *disempowering questions*, focusing on outcomes you don't want, so your body is going to react with the fight, flight, or freeze syndrome. Things will start to happen physically: your palms or forehead will start to sweat; your breath will become shallow; you can't think clearly; your stomach might even go into knots. These reactions are controlled by your reptile brain, which is telling you that *this is a dangerous situation, and you should run!*

Of course, you can't run, because this is your job. So what should you do in situations like this?

Landing the Deal

Remember Bobby Knight's quote: "The key to being a champion is NOT 'the will to win.' What makes a champion is the will to PREPARE to win."

How do you prepare to win in situations like this? The key is being *value-centric* to others.

Let's take the classic example of a single guy in a bar, hoping to get a date. Most guys would be looking for what they can get in the situation. Of course, it's not wrong to want to get something from any social interaction (indeed it's nearly impossible for us humans to not want to get something), but the question comes down to the old saying, "What you focus on, grows."

If you are constantly focused on what you want and what you need, you are really focusing on what you *don't* have. And when you focus on what you don't have, what do you get more of? The experience of *not* having!

Conversely, if you simply switch your outlook from "What can I *get*?" to "What can I *give*?" and "What value can I bring to this situation?" your mind will start to focus on what you *have*.

If you go around believing, "I don't have," then God will show you all the reasons you *don't have*.

If you believe, "I don't have enough money," you will find all the reasons you don't have enough money.

If you believe, "I don't have enough time," you will find all the reasons you don't have enough time.

If you believe, "It's hard to get ahead," you will find all the reasons it's hard to get ahead.

If, however, you believe, "I am enough," and "I have enough," you will find all the reasons that you are, in fact, enough and that you do have enough.

To go back to our example, what if that guy at the bar stopped being the guy looking for something to get and started being the guy looking to add value to the people around him? How would that change his mood, his emotions, his thinking, his focus, and his level of self-confidence? This is what the people with unstoppable

THIS IS WHY I'M ON A MISSION TO ERADICATE NOT-ENOUGHNESS.

self-confidence are unconsciously doing—believing that *they are enough* and coming from a place of being value-centric to others.

Becoming a Value Magnet

I'm sure you've met people that you were drawn to for some unexplainable reason. And it isn't only the ones with classic good looks that fall into this category. Haven't you ever met someone to whom you felt drawn, as if by an invisible magnet?

The fact is that we humans are magnets. Our bodies are made up of cells; cells are made of molecules; molecules are made of atoms; and atoms are essentially energy. In short, you and I and every person you will ever meet is a walking magnet.

Every magnet has two poles: positive and negative. Isn't it fascinating that we use these words to describe magnets, just as we often use them to describe people?

We human beings are drawn to other human beings while at the same time being repelled by others. Just like a magnet, right now you are attracting some people and repelling others.

That's why one of the Power Habits of Unstoppable Self-Confidence is to become aware of, and make conscious choices about, exactly whom you are attracting and whom you are repelling.

We've all heard phrases like "Like attracts like" and "Birds of a feather flock together." These are examples of the law of magnetism—the fact that you and I and everyone you meet are actual magnets, who are attracting certain people and repelling others.

THESE ARE EXAMPLES OF THE LAW OF MAGNETISM.

What about the phrase "Opposites attract"? As we all know, when you try to connect poles of a magnet that are the same polarity, they will push each other apart. And you and I can think of many examples of couples who seem to be nothing alike who nonetheless seem to get along swimmingly.

I believe the reason for this is simple: If we were to look beneath the surface, we would find that what really keeps those couples together is a deep shared love of something in common—perhaps their children, their faith, their work, or something else that bonds them together.

Being Value-Centric to Others

This idea goes back to being value-centric to others. This does not mean letting people walk all over you and giving them everything they want with no regard for what *you* want. Nothing could be further from the truth.

When you come into any situation, meeting, or conversation seeking to add value to the other party, it will be very hard for that person to dislike you. Think about it: if someone is trying to help you get what you want, are you going to fight them? Are you going to dislike someone who is trying to help you get what you want? It's not very likely.

Of course, that does not mean you just give everyone what they want with no regard for what you want. Being value-centric to others goes back to Stephen Covey's principle: "Seek first to understand, then to be understood."

After coaching thousands of people, I have observed that most people do not understand their own value. As a result, they are going around constantly focused on what they can get from others.

BY BEING VALUE-CENTRIC, YOU REALIZE YOUR OWN VALUE.

But what if you became the one person in a million who is focused on what you can bring to the situation? Actually, that is the word I prefer to use with my clients: rather than the word *give*, I advise my clients to use the word *bring*.

Let's say you're going over to a friend's house for dinner. Do you *give* something, or do you *bring* something? When you bring something, all of you will get to partake of it, whether it's a bottle of wine or some potato salad. When you bring something to a situation, meeting, or conversation, you don't just give it; you also get to enjoy it and partake of it. Which, I have found, makes it easier for most of us to focus on *bringing*.

Becoming Your Best Self

I would never coach someone *not* to be themselves. The Power Habits of Unstoppable Self-Confidence is not about changing who you are or having to become the life of the party if that's not who you really are. It is about realizing that you are enough and taking new actions to remind yourself of that fact.

One of the great ironies of this work, then, is that most of what we have to do is not to learn but to *unlearn* disempowering habits that most of us developed years or decades ago.

That's why it's my hope and belief that you will use these strategies to add more value to the world by revealing who you really are in a way that benefits yourself as well as other people.

Be sure to keep reading, because next we'll examine the secret of the "naturals" that's hidden in plain sight—plus specific, actionable ways to build your unstoppable self-confidence, starting right now.

7

My CLEAR Formula to Unleash Your Inner Superhero

Courage is resistance to fear,
mastery of fear, not absence of fear.

—MARK TWAIN

In the fall of 1958, a couple from Bowling Green, Ohio, decided to adopt a six-week-old son. At the age of two, however, the boy contracted a mysterious disease that caused him to stop growing. After numerous tests and several incorrect diagnoses, including a diagnosis of cystic fibrosis that gave him just six months to live, the couple took their son to Boston's Children's Hospital, where his mysterious ailment began to correct itself with the aid of a special diet and moderate exercise.

Soon the boy felt well enough to watch as his older sister went ice skating, and he decided to try ice skating for himself. From the beginning, the boy skated with great confidence and uncommon speed.

He began taking formal lessons and joined a hockey team. Within a year, his illness disappeared, and he began growing again—although, for the rest of his life, he would always be smaller than his peers. His miraculous recovery was attributed to intense physical activity in the cold atmosphere of the ice rink.

At the age of thirteen, the boy began training with Pierre Brunet, a former Olympic champion. But in 1976, he was almost forced to quit skating because of his family's financial struggles and the high cost of training. He decided to enroll at Bowling Green State University, thinking his dream of being an Olympic skater was over before it had begun. Just before classes began, however, an anonymous couple who had supported other Olympic hopefuls volunteered to sponsor the boy, and he immediately resumed his training.

Over the next several years, his continued dedication and hard work paid off. By 1980, he placed third in the United States National competition and won a berth on the U.S. Olympic squad, earning a solid fifth-place finish at the 1980 Winter Olympics in Lake Placid, New York. In March 1981, his free-skate program at the World Championships enabled him to overtake heavily favored fellow countryman David Santee and Igor Bobrin of the Soviet Union to win the title: he was only the second American to do so since 1970. He went on to win sixteen consecutive championships, and at the 1984 Winter Olympics in Sarajevo he was heavily favored to win gold.

And that's exactly what Scott Hamilton did.

A month later, Scott went on to victory at the World Championships in Ottawa, Canada, and turned pro in April 1984, instantly becoming one of the sport's most popular performers, which he remains to this day.

But life hasn't exactly been easy for Scott Hamilton. Even after his Olympic victory and securing his spot in the hearts of millions of fans worldwide, TV executives and promoters still believed that only female figure skaters could draw a big audience. After he had starred in the Ice Capades for two years, a sudden change of ownership led to his abrupt dismissal.

Frustrated with the lack of commercial opportunities for male figure skaters, Hamilton created his own professional ice revue, The Scott Hamilton America Tour, which evolved into the touring spectacle Stars on Ice. He single-handedly revolutionized the role of the male figure skater with his magnetic personality, sense of humor, and showmanship, which helped create a vast new TV audience for figure skating.

After twelve years of unsuccessfully pitching proposals to skeptical TV executives, Scott finally won the first in a series of prime-time network television specials. He won the first professional world figure skating championship in 1984 and again in 1986, and in 1990 was inducted into the U.S. Olympic Hall of Fame.

What Is a Superhero?

It has often been said that the true test of a person's character is not what they achieve but what they overcome. Certainly stories like Scott Hamilton's prove that. His enduring popularity is evidence that, even as spectators, we can appreciate what someone like him had to overcome to reach the pinnacle of his profession.

Which leads us to the question: what does it mean to be a hero, and can *any* of us become one?

To answer this question, I'd like to take a light-hearted look at how different things were when I was growing up. When I graduated from high school in the mideighties, to admit that you were into superheroes and comic books was the equivalent of social suicide. While no one under the age of twenty-five would believe this today, to admit that you were into things like Spider-Man or X-Men or Captain America would be to guarantee that you would never get a date with a girl!

Fast-forward to today, and nearly every other weekend features a new Hollywood blockbuster starring the superheroes that I grew up reading (including many that even I, the nerdiest nerd in the industry, had never heard of!).

Nowadays you can't walk down the street or turn on the television without seeing people of all ages wearing their favorite T-shirts from Marvel Comics, Star Trek, Star Wars, or even—that nerdiest of nerdvana—Doctor Who. (Yes, I was into Doctor Who in the eighties).

Back then, to be labeled a nerd or geek was definitely uncool, and I was both. Today, people proudly hang those labels on themselves—and in the most ironic twist, it is now cooler to be a nerd than not to be!

SUPERHEROES ARE EVERYWHERE TODAY.

Sometimes it takes a while for society to come around and accept different points of view. Being a hero when I was growing up meant being a star athlete and . . . well, that's about it.

Today, however, heroism has more meanings than it ever did before. A hero can be someone who helps others in their time of need. A hero can be someone who donates to charity or volunteers at their church. A hero can be a person who puts the needs of others ahead of themselves.

I'd also like to point out how views toward the military and those who serve in our armed forces have changed a great deal in the last twenty-five years. When I was growing up in the early seventies, America was still grieving over painful events like Vietnam, Watergate, and the assassinations of JFK, RFK, and Martin Luther King Jr. While I'm too young to really remember those events, I do remember when I was growing up that there was always a strong distrust for the military. But today people in the armed forces are treated like the heroes they are and have always been. I'm grateful to see these brave men and women get the respect and admiration that they have always deserved. In fact, Babette and I are often in airports as we travel to and from my keynote speeches or private workshops, across the country and around the world. She has a habit of going up to every man or woman she sees wearing a military uniform, giving them a big hug, and saying, "Thank you for serving."

While there are many definitions for what it means to be a hero, I suggest that unleashing your inner superhero boils down to two essential things:

1. A deep inner acceptance of who you really are.

2. An unwavering commitment to add value to everyone you meet.

How Do You Bring Value?

Here are two questions that I encourage my coaching clients to ask whenever they're entering a social encounter: What can I bring to this situation? And what value can I add to the people I'm talking to?

I think these two questions form the basis of being superheroic, because it is almost impossible to be needy when you are asking these questions.

Here is one method I teach my coaching clients to help them eradicate neediness: *the CLEAR formula to unleash your inner superhero.*

C: Come from Enough

One of my favorite stories about someone who mastered the art of how to come from enough is Harrison Ford. When he arrived in Hollywood, he was appalled at how poorly actors were treated, particularly ones who were out of work. So he decided that he would never have to depend on acting work in order to survive. He went to the library, read books on carpentry, and taught himself how to become a master carpenter. Soon he was building furniture for famous people like George Lucas and Steven Spielberg. When he went to auditions, if he was offered a role for $500, he would say things like, "$500? I can make that in a weekend building a bookshelf!" And he would turn down roles that didn't feel right to him.

Is it any wonder that he went on to become one of the biggest movie stars of all time, with his films grossing over $20 billion worldwide?

By the way, Ford has stated numerous times in interviews that he first got into acting class in his senior year of high school "to get over his shyness." No kidding!

HARRISON FORD IS A GREAT EXAMPLE OF HOW TO COME FROM ENOUGH

L: Learn What Makes Them Thirsty

You've heard the saying, "You can lead a horse to water, but you can't make him drink"? I like to tell my coaching clients: "You can if you know what makes him thirsty!"

People don't do what you want them to do; they do something because they want to do it for themselves. So how do you learn what makes someone thirsty? By speaking directly to their reptile brain, which is focused on the most basic needs of survival; it determines whether things in your environment should be treated as dangerous or safe.

THIS IS HOW TO SPEAK TO SOMEONE'S REPTILE BRAIN.

Therefore, when you learn what makes your prospect thirsty, you demonstrate that what you're proposing is simple and safe and will give them exactly what they want with a minimum of work on their part. That is music to the reptile brain's ears.

This step means doing your research ahead of time. You can't always count on people coming out and telling you what they want or need. In most negotiations, the other party won't tell you or will even try to mislead you. As a result, you need to prepare your argument and anticipate what the other party wants before you ever set foot in the conference room or go on a virtual meeting. This will give you the confidence to speak your mind and present your case without being needy.

E: Earn Respect by Demonstrating High Value

No one does anything until and unless they perceive there is a benefit to themselves in doing it.

This step boils down to how essential it is to be value-centric to others. As we've already seen, it's nearly impossible to be needy and value-centric to others at the same time.

Think about it: the definition of being needy is that you need or desire something from someone else in order to feel good enough.

But if you are constantly asking questions like, "What can I bring to this situation?" it will be nearly impossible for your brain to process that as neediness, because someone who brings something necessarily has to *have* something to bring.

That's why, when you ask these kinds of empowering questions, you flip the polarity of your inner magnet from neediness to unstoppable self-confidence.

A: Ask for What You Want without Attachment

Up until this step, you've focused solely on coming from enough and demonstrating high value to the other party. In this step, you are going to ask for what you want, but in a very specific way: you're going to ask *without caring if the other person gives it to you.*

I know this sounds counterintuitive, because in traditional success programs, we've been taught to ask for what we want and keep asking until we get it.

While that's not necessarily wrong, after studying the naturals of success for so many years, I came to realize that one of their most powerful secret weapons is their ability to *not care* if the other party says yes or not—which, paradoxically, greatly increases the chances that the other party will give you what you want!

Think back to negotiations that you've been in, where the person on the other side of the table was asking you for something and *really cared* if you gave it to them. You can actually feel that kind of pressure, can't you? This speaks to the fact that our reptile brains, which have been trained over millions of years to detect threats to our safety, are uncannily good at sensing when something doesn't quite feel right.

That's why this fourth step of my formula involves doing two things at once: asking for what you want, while simultaneously completely letting go of your need for the other party to give it to you. It sounds harsh, but one of the realities of modern negotiation is that the person who cares the least usually wins. Which leads us to . . .

R: Relax by Remembering You Can't Control the Outcome

After many years of experience and making every mistake in the book, I've realized that one of the easiest ways to eradicate neediness and achieve unstoppable self-confidence is to remember that *you are not in charge.*

No matter how smart, clever, persuasive, or cool you are, you simply cannot make other people do what you want them to do unless they decide they want to do it for themselves. Ultimately you can't control whether someone buys from you or not, any more than you can control whether someone falls in love with you.

Although you can't control outcomes, you *can* control what you do. You can't control other people's behavior, but you can certainly influence it. There is a big difference between control and influence. In fact, you are influencing other people's behavior all the time, whether you're aware of it or not.

Control seeks to enforce behavior through strict rules and penalties, while influence inspires positive change through understanding, collaboration, and empowerment. For example, imagine you are a team leader in a workplace setting, and you have two employees who consistently arrive late to meetings. You can choose to either control or influence their behavior. A controlling approach might involve threats and punishments, leading to compliance out of fear. On the other hand, an influential approach involves open dialogue, empathy, and finding mutually beneficial solutions, motivating individuals to change willingly and fostering stronger relationships.

The key distinction between control and influence lies in their approach to behavior change. Control relies on enforcement, fear, and external pressure, often resulting in compliance but strained relationships. Influence, on the other hand, prioritizes understanding, collaboration, and empowerment, fostering genuine engagement and motivation. By embracing influence, we create an environment where individuals willingly embrace change, leading to sustainable transformations and stronger connections.

That's why, when you follow my CLEAR formula to unleash your inner superhero, you will greatly increase your chances of getting more of what you want: you will have eliminated neediness and cleared one of the biggest blocks to unstoppable self-confidence.

Eradicating neediness ultimately means that you stop trying to control everything and everyone else. This will greatly lower your stress level instantly. As you let go of outcomes and stop caring so much about what other people think, you'll find that your level of self-confidence naturally increases. After all, it takes a lot of mental and emotional energy to try and control everyone and everything, which you can't do anyway.

If you follow my CLEAR formula, you may not be able to leap tall buildings in a single bound, but you'll find yourself standing taller, breathing easier, and feeling much better about the value you bring to others and to the world.

In the next chapter, we'll examine how to turn worry and fear into self-confidence and success. I'll also give you one of my best secrets for increasing your self-confidence and making procrastination a thing of the past.

8

How to Turn Worry and Fear into Self-Confidence and Success

Inaction breeds doubt and fear. Action breeds confidence and courage. If you want to conquer fear, do not sit home and think about it. Go out and get busy.

—DALE CARNEGIE

In the summer of 1930, a young man and his wife living in the Midwest welcomed their second child into the world, a son. After the father was elected to Congress in 1942, the family moved to Washington, D.C.

As a child, the boy showed avid interest in making and saving money. He would go door to door selling Coca-Cola and chewing gum and worked in his grandfather's grocery store. While still in high school, he earned money delivering newspapers, selling golf balls and stamps, and washing cars.

In his sophomore year of high school, he and a friend spent $25 to buy a used pinball machine, which they set up in a local barber shop. Within months, they had placed several machines in barber shops around the neighborhood. Upon graduation from Woodrow Wilson High School in 1947, his senior yearbook photo read: "Likes math, a future stockbroker."

When the young man entered the Wharton School of Business in 1947, he found himself having to give speeches to the class. This is when the fear of public speaking hit the young Warren Buffett for the first time.

Today we all know Warren Buffett as one of the world's richest men. Not only is he one of the world's most-quoted individuals, but he also speaks every year in front of more than 20,000 raving fans who flock to the annual meeting of his company, Berkshire Hathaway.

Yet Buffett admits that at that point in his life, he was absolutely "terrified" of public speaking. In fact, he says that he was so afraid of speaking in front of people that he would arrange his college classes to avoid having to get up in front of the class.

Realizing that he had to get over his fear, Buffett enrolled in a public speaking course, then promptly dropped out before the class started. "I lost my nerve," he says today.

At the age of twenty-one, Buffett began his career in the securities industry. He realized that in order to reach his full potential, he had to master the skill and overcome his fear of public speaking.

Buffett enrolled in a Dale Carnegie course with thirty other people who, like him, were "terrified of getting up and saying our names in front of people." That course changed his life, because it was through the practice of speaking in front of that group of thirty people that he overcame his fear and went on to become "the Oracle of Omaha."

Today Buffett is quoted as saying, "You've got to be able to communicate in life, and it's enormously important. Schools, to some extent, underemphasize that. If you can't communicate and talk to other people and get your ideas across, you're giving up on your potential."

Other famous people who have reported having a fear of public speaking include Bruce Willis, Julia Roberts, Jimmy Stewart, James Earl Jones, Samuel L. Jackson, and even one of the greatest orators in history, Winston Churchill, who often described himself as having a "speech impediment." So if you are one of the millions of people afflicted with the fear of public speaking, you're in great company!

Books and courses on overcoming the fear of public speaking are in constant demand. In fact, according to a Gallup poll, the only thing that adults fear more than speaking in front of a group is snakes, which makes the fear of public speaking the second-most common fear of American men and women. Another survey showed that the fear of death was number six, which means that most people would rather die three times than speak in public!

Millions of people are afflicted with the fear of public speaking. What, then, causes this fear—and if speaking in public really is as important as Warren Buffett says, how can we turn this common fear into self-confidence and success?

The Ancient Cause of the Fear of Public Speaking

In the ancient past, human beings lived in a world with many life-threatening risks, like large predators and starvation. Because our earliest ancestors had to overcome these problems just to survive, they decided to live in groups; that way, group members could alert one another to predators and other dangers and fight them off. Living in groups also provides many survival advantages, which is why early humans and other large primates evolved to be social creatures, and why we humans developed social structures and hierarchies that remain to this day.

Because early humans didn't have claws or sharp teeth and weren't particularly fast or strong compared to the predators they faced, they survived primarily by their ability to collaborate. Those that got along with their fellow tribesmen and were part of the social structure were the most likely to survive. Those who didn't get along well with the group or broke tribal customs were usually banished from the tribe.

This is what causes the fear of public speaking. In many ancient tribes, banishment from the tribe was seen as a fate worse than death, because there was little chance that you were going to survive out there on your own.

The word *contribute* has its roots in the fourteenth century and is derived from the word *tribe*. *Contribute* means *to bring together or add*. How amazing that the very words we've been discussing in this book—*contribute, bring, add*—involve some of the most ancient ideas we have as a species.

Because we humans are social creatures, we are wired to fear or feel threatened by anything that might threaten our social status. Therefore, the fear of public speaking has at its roots the fear of banishment from the tribe, the fear of ostracism by other members of the group.

According to Kip Williams, a professor of psychological sciences at Purdue who has studied ostracism, it "appears to occur in all social animals that have been observed in nature." Williams says, "To my knowledge, in the animal kingdom, ostracism is not only a form of social death, it also results in death. The animal is unable to protect itself against predators, cannot garner enough food, etc., and usually dies within a short period of time."

So when you're about to go in front of a group and deliver your speech, your ancient reptile brain will probably be going nuts for this very reason. It's telling you something like this: *"Hey, if you mess this up or say something stupid, you're going to be banished from the tribe, which means we're gonna die!"*

In short, the fear of public speaking really is the fear of being rejected, which is the fear of being banished from the tribe, and ultimately the fear of death.

My APPLAUSE Method

The great news is that I've helped hundreds of my coaching clients to turn the fear of public speaking—indeed, nearly any fear or worry—into self-confidence and success.

Because I love acronyms, I call it Dr. Noah's APPLAUSE Method for Turning Worry and Fear into Self-Confidence and Success. Here's what APPLAUSE stands for.

A: Admit What You're Really Scared Of

Many people don't overcome their fears because they don't realize or admit what's causing them.

As we've just seen, the fear of public speaking really comes from the fear of rejection. But even that is not the real fear. The real fear is that if you're rejected, you'll be banished from the tribe and die alone in the wilderness.

I know that might sound hard to believe, but your reptile brain evolved millions of years ago and still hasn't gotten the memo that we're not living in tribal days any more. That's why the fear of public speaking affects so many people: the fear of being banished strikes at the heart of what it means to be human: to be accepted and to be part of a group.

And let's be honest. When we fear public speaking, we're really afraid that people won't like us. It is perfectly natural to want other people to like us. We would hardly be human if we didn't. But because most people don't admit what they're

> **THE FEAR OF BEING BANISHED IS WHAT YOU'RE REALLY SCARED OF.**

really afraid of, they can't overcome their fear. Yet as Warren Buffett has said, when you base your decisions on whether people like you or not, you are going to have great difficulties in reaching your full potential.

Therefore, the first step of my APPLAUSE Method is to *admit what you're really scared of.*

Two P's: Practice and Prepare to Win

It's not enough to simply picture good things happening or imagine the best possible outcome. (If that's all it took, every person who ever dreamed of playing football would have won the Super Bowl.) You must also *practice* by doing things in real life. This means you must do the one thing that most people aren't willing do, and that is prepare to win.

While everyone has the will to win, very few have the will to prepare to win.

I can't think of a better way to overcome the fear of public speaking than to join Toastmasters International. Toastmasters International was founded by a man named Ralph Smedley at the YMCA in Santa Ana, California, in 1924. Since that time, more than four million people have been members of Toastmasters, and today the organization serves nearly 300,000 members in over 120 countries through its more than 14,000 member clubs.

Back in 1997, when I launched my company, SuccessClinic.com, from my college dorm room, I realized that I needed to master the skill of public speaking. I went to my local Toastmasters Club in Northampton, Massachusetts, and decided to join. Shortly thereafter, I became the president of the Northampton Toastmasters Club. It was one of the best decisions I ever made—not only for my career, but also for my life. Speaking at Toastmasters taught me critical skills that would serve me for the rest of my life—like how to think on your feet, how to give and receive positive feedback, how to organize your thoughts, how to form an argument and present your case to an audience, and many more.

That's just one of the many reasons that whenever clients come to me asking how they can not just improve their public speaking skills, but also increase their self-confidence and communication skills, I recommend that they join Toastmasters and go through their Competent Communicator or Competent Leader programs. Just go to toastmasters.org and find a club near you.

I CAN'T THINK OF A BETTER WAY TO OVERCOME THE FEAR OF PUBLIC SPEAKING THAN TO JOIN TOASTMASTERS.

L: Let Go of the Outcome

Now this sounds counterintuitive, but after you have practiced and prepared to win, you must *let go* of the outcome. What do I mean by that?

Think about a time when you really wanted something. Can you think about how you felt when you wanted that thing so badly that you stopped yourself from getting it? In sports, this phenomenon is called *choking*. We've all seen examples of great athletes who snatched defeat from the jaws of victory: they were just about to win the championship or the medal, when they did something so inexplicably bone-headed that they ended up losing the tournament, the medal, or the game.

This is undoubtedly the most frustrating aspect of sports—and indeed of life: when you know you were in a position to win, and suddenly the victory was snatched away from you. Yet what's even worse is when *you* are the one who snatched the victory away from yourself, simply because you wanted it too much!

That's why this step of my method is essential. After you practice and prepare to win, you must do something that sounds totally counterintuitive, and that is to *let go* of the outcome. Looking back on my life, I understand the truth of something Mark Twain wrote: "I have known a great many troubles in my life, most of which never happened." Paul McCartney wrote the famous Beatles song "Let It Be" after he had a dream in which his late mother came to him during a particularly difficult time in his life. In the dream, Paul's mother told him to let things be and they would turn out all right in the end.

The more we try to control outcomes, the less we can control them. Not only that, but the less happy we are and the less self-confident we feel.

> THE MORE WE TRY TO CONTROL OUTCOMES, THE LESS CONTROL WE HAVE.

When we look at it in this light, letting go is not a sign of weakness, but a sign of turning fear and anxiety into self-confidence and success. Paradoxically, only by letting go of our need to control can we find the peace, freedom, and self-confidence to live the best lives we can.

The Second A: Accept the Worst That Could Happen

In Dale Carnegie's classic book *How to Stop Worrying and Start Living,* he tells the story of Willis H. Carrier, the inventor of the modern air conditioner and founder of the Carrier Corporation. Early in his career, Mr. Carrier worked for the Buffalo Forge Company in

Buffalo, New York, where he was responsible for installing a new gas-cleaning device in one of their plants in Missouri. Unfortunately, the installation was not going well, and the company seemed likely to lose $20,000—over half a million dollars in today's money!

Carrier said it felt as though someone had struck him in the head; his insides began to twist and turn, and he became so worried that he couldn't sleep. He finally came up with a three-step method to handle his worry problem that Dale Carnegie eventually called "The Willis Carrier Formula."

Step 1. *Analyze the situation fearlessly and honestly, and figure out what is the worst that could possibly happen.*

Carrier realized that no one was going to jail him or shoot him. But he acknowledged that his employers might have to replace the machinery and lose the $20,000 they had invested, which would look bad on his record and probably get him fired.

Step 2. *Reconcile yourself to accepting the worst that could possibly happen.*

In other words, emotionally accept that the worst has happened and that you now have to face the reality of that awful situation. Carrier resolved to accept that his employer might indeed lose the money and he might indeed be fired. He then revealed the "secret sauce" of his magic formula for reducing worry:

Step 3. *After identifying the worst that could happen and mentally accepting that the worst has happened, calmly devote yourself to improving on the worst, which you have already mentally accepted.*

Carrier explained how he then tried to figure out ways of reducing the loss of money that the company now faced. He ran several tests and discovered that if the company spent another $5,000 for additional equipment, their problem would be solved. They did this, and instead of losing $20,000, the company made $15,000—a handsome profit of over $400,000 in today's money!

Carnegie quotes Carrier as saying: "I probably would never have been able to figure out this solution if I had kept on worrying; because one of the worst features about worrying is that it destroys our ability to concentrate. When we worry, our minds jump here and there and everywhere, and we lose all power of decision. However, when we force ourselves to face the worst and accept it mentally, we eliminate all those vague imaginings and put ourselves in a position in which we are able to concentrate on solving our problem."

CARRIER'S METHOD WILL HELP YOU OVERCOME THE FEAR OF MAKING THE WRONG DECISION.

What Carnegie and Carrier knew intuitively, and that modern

science now shows conclusively, is that worry and fear take us out of the moment and sap our ability to make good decisions. Why? Again, it's your reptile brain and neocortex at work. When we go into worry mode—which is simply another form of fight, flight, or freeze—the reptile brain takes over and we actually *can't think straight*. But when we apply this simple method, we actively flip the "on" switch in our neocortex—which, as we now know, is designed for problem solving, communication, and other higher brain functions.

In short, I highly recommend this simple formula for turning worry and fear into self-confidence and success.

Which brings us to the U in my APPLAUSE Method.

U: Understand Your Audience's Point of View

Whether you're speaking on stage in front of thousands or in your employer's office, talking to one, you will often be trying to convince another human being to do what you want them to do. In fact, getting people to do what you want them to do is the goal of every sales, marketing, persuasion, leadership, management, relationship, and communication book, program, and seminar that has ever been created.

Whether you're trying to get a raise, get a date, get your teenager to clean their room, or get that whale of a prospect to become a whale of a client, you will always want certain outcomes in nearly every social or business setting.

Although billions of words have been spoken and written on this subject, I suggest that every argument you could ever make for getting other people to do what you want them to do comes down to this one basic truth:

The best way to get someone to do what you want them to do is make it in THEIR best interest to do it.

Dictators, generals, and despots over the centuries have tried to make other people do what they wanted them to do, without the people's consent. Over time, every one of them has failed, no matter the size of their armies or the amount of power they used. If it didn't work for them, what makes us think it will work for us?

Ultimately, the only way to get the results you want—whether it's a promotion, a date, a spouse, or a client—is to have the other person *want* to do it for themselves.

That's why this step involves taking the time to discover what the other party wants and then showing them how doing what you want them to do will help them get what *they* want.

This step is simple to articulate, but it may be the hardest to take. While most of us are very good at understanding what we want, it's often difficult to put ourselves in a position to understand what someone else wants.

Which leads to the S in my APPLAUSE Method.

S: Speak to Your Audience's Needs and Wants

Remember, you're not going to get anyone to do what you want them to do because you want them to do it. They will only do it if they decide for themselves that they want to do it, because it is in their best interest to do it.

If you walk into a meeting or presentation without understanding your prospect's point of view, you will indeed be in the position of hoping for the best. However, that will always put you in a position of lower value.

Instead, you're going to find out what your prospect wants, and then speak to their wants in a way that makes sense to them.

For example, many years ago, I was still a struggling author who had been in the business for a while but hadn't really broken through to mainstream success. I had built a kind of cult following of people around the world who really believed in me and my message because it had helped them in their lives. But I hadn't been offered a publishing deal with a major book publisher, which I really wanted.

One day, a friend introduced me to one of the top literary agents, a whip-smart and well-connected man named Steve who, it seemed, knew or had worked with everyone in the publishing industry.

I ended up hiring Steve as my literary agent, and he began shopping my book manuscript to the big New York publishers. A few weeks later, he arranged for a tour where he and I would meet with the decision-makers at the biggest publishing houses in New York.

This was the dream that I had been hoping for! I couldn't believe that it was finally happening. But I started to get nervous and worry about what might happen if things didn't go the way I wanted them to. I began losing sleep, and my stomach was in knots all the time.

Finally, I remembered my own method, and after following these steps, I immediately relaxed and started sleeping like a baby again.

When I got to New York, my agent warned me that our very first meeting would be with the second largest publisher in the world, and that we would be meeting with all the company's executives and vice presidents. "Great!" I said. "Nothing like starting the season with the Super Bowl!"

Sure enough, at our first meeting, I walked into a boardroom with the president of the publishing company, the vice president of sales, vice president of marketing, vice president of publicity, and about a dozen other high-ranking executives.

But I was so relaxed and confident by that point that I *forgot to be nervous!* I had done so much research and had prepared for that moment for so long, it was as if I had been doing it my whole life.

When one executive asked me a question, I calmly answered the question with facts and without embellishment. When another pointed out that my sales weren't that high, I said, "Exactly! That's the problem!" and went on to explain how we were going to fix it with our new marketing strategy.

Out of the corner of my eye, I noticed my agent sitting quietly with a little smile on his face. He didn't say much and didn't interrupt me once, so I had to assume that I was doing all right.

After that first meeting ended, my agent and I got into a taxi to go to our next meeting. I asked him, "So how did I do?" I had no idea if I had just blown it, because I had no prior experience to go on.

He looked at me and said, "Noah, you hit it out of the park!"

It turned out that that first meeting was indeed the biggest one of the more than dozen meetings we had with publishers over the next forty-eight hours. And that publishing company, HarperCollins, ended up offering me a six-figure advance for my first hardcover mass market book, entitled *The Secret Code of Success,* which went on to be published in over a dozen different languages around the world.

THIS IS HOW I GOT A HIGH SIX-FIGURE PUBLISHING DEAL.

The point of the story? When you follow my APPLAUSE Method, sometimes you'll amaze even yourself!

And what does the E in APPLAUSE stand for? I bet you thought I forgot, didn't you? No, I didn't: I just wanted to make sure you were paying attention!

E: End with a Call to Action

You've understood your listener's point of view, you've given your powerful presentation, and you've spoken to their needs and wants. What now?

Many people forget to give a clear call to action, because they figure that people will just know what to do. Yet that's not good enough! It is not enough to simply leave it in your audience's hands to somehow magically know the steps you want them to take.

At this point, if you've done everything I've suggested, you probably have your listeners saying to themselves, "I really want to do this. What do you want me to do now?"

You know what you want them to do now, but how are they supposed to know unless you tell them? In this final step, you simply say to them: *"So, if you're ready to move forward, here's what to do now."*

Before I learned this, I would give amazing stage presentations, yet never make any sales. It was the most frustrating thing in the world! People would come up to me and say, "Noah, I loved your speech!" And I would say, "Thanks!" But they never bought anything!

One day, I was speaking at an event in Florida and only one person signed up out of a group of 100. I was terribly disappointed. After the event, the organizer, who was British, came up to me, put his arm around me and said, "Noah, you are an amazing speaker. But you're rubbish at selling."

He showed me that because I hadn't told my audience *how* to buy my program, they simply didn't know what they were supposed to do. Once I started ending my presentations with a simple, specific call to action, my closing percentage went from 1 percent to 20, 50, even 70 percent!

Giving people a call to action means that you are coming from enough: you are not being needy; in fact, you're demonstrating the self-confidence that comes from knowing that what you're offering has real value.

THIS IS HOW I CLOSE 30–70 PERCENT FROM STAGE

My clients and I have used my APPLAUSE Method hundreds of times, and we've found it to be a highly effective way to stop worrying and simply be in the moment—which means you can make better decisions and have increased self-confidence and a much greater chance of success.

In the next chapter, I'll reveal what I call the *eight eroders of self-confidence*, which you must avoid at all costs. Then I'll end with a final call to action to help you get the most out of this book.

9

The Final Frontier: Embracing the Freedom to Be Who You Really Are

*Envy comes from people's ignorance of,
or lack of belief in, their own gifts.*

—JEAN VANIER

In this next-to-last chapter, I'm going to share with you the *eight eroders of self-confidence* and show you why you must avoid these corrosive behaviors at all costs. They will not only damage your self-confidence but will hold you back from the success you're capable of. Ultimately they could hold you back from being and expressing who you really are.

We often follow habits and engage in behaviors that will slowly but surely erode our self-confidence.

An eroder of self-confidence is a habit or behavior that erodes, destroys, or damages our self-confidence.

Here are the eight eroders of self-confidence.

1. The Fear of Criticism

From my work over the last twenty-five years, I've discovered that the fear of criticism stops more people from pursuing their dreams than almost anything else.

As you know, I started my company, SuccessClinic.com, in my college dorm room way back in 1997. I didn't know it at the time, but we were the first personal growth and mental health coaching company founded completely online. Indeed, I believe that the Internet is the single greatest communication tool ever invented. It took less than ten years for it to go from being something no one had ever heard of to the most dominant form of human communication the world has ever known. I believe that is partly because it is the first form of human communication that is readily available to nearly anyone on planet earth. That fact is the good news and the bad news about the Internet.

The Internet is good because it has allowed regular people like you and me to start our own businesses and build financial freedom. When I launched SuccessClinic.com in my dorm room, I had less than $800 to my name. Yet within a matter of months, people around the world were buying my programs—many from countries I had never even heard of! I could never have

THIS IS WHY THE INTERNET IS THE MOST POWERFUL COMMUNICATION PLATFORM EVER INVENTED.

reached those clients and customers around the globe without the Internet.

Along with the good, we have to face the not-so-good. Because the Internet makes global communication so fast, cheap, and easy, we have seen the rise of a disturbing trend that has never existed before—online bullying.

There is no way to avoid the fact that when you start to express who you really are, people will criticize you. They will say things about you in such a way as to cause the greatest possible pain, hurt, and embarrassment. We used to call this "talking behind people's backs"—because talking was the principal form of communication back then. Now, because of the Internet, people aren't even bothering to talk behind your back—they do it right in front of you, probably on your Facebook page!

Psychologists call this phenomenon the *online disinhibition effect.* This is a loosening (or complete abandonment) of social inhibitions during online interactions that would be present in normal face-to-face communication. As a result, some users may actually become more affectionate, more willing to open up to others, and less guarded about emotions. On the other hand, many Internet users frequently do or say harmful things without fear of reprisal. The website overcomebullying.org states that with "the advent of modern communications such as email, chat, text messaging and cell phones as well as the ability to publish online on websites, blogs and social networking sites, the bully's reach and powers of social manipulation have been increased exponentially." The site suggests that perhaps "the internet lends itself to this indifference. Bullies don't have to see their victims or answer for their actions."

As a result, those of us who are trying to make the world a better place may face the possibility of cyberbullying. I've read numerous articles on big-name celebrities who have stated that they have banned themselves from Googling their own names, because they have realized that they will inevitably run across dozens or hundreds of websites saying nasty things about them.

Criticism always hurts, even if it's posted online by people you don't know and who don't know you. If celebrities aren't immune to the pain of criticism, why should you and I be any different? The more successful you become, the more trolls will come out of the woodwork to try and tear you down. That's why you must learn to deal with criticism, because the more successful you get, the more you will be criticized.

That brings us to the second eroder of self-confidence:

2. Neediness

I wrote in an earlier chapter about the need to overcome neediness as one of the most important Power Habits of Unstoppable Self-Confidence. And it's true: nothing will erode your self-confidence faster than neediness. The saddest part is that it essentially ensures that you won't get the very thing you need. You and I and everyone you will ever meet want approval from other people. We all need loving support and encouragement to become who we really are; yet if you are needy in your approach to getting it, it will probably ensure that you won't.

It goes back to the old saying, "It's not what you say, it's how you say it." When you eliminate neediness, you no longer have to play games, remember fancy lines, or use prewritten scripts. You can learn how to talk with anyone, anytime, anywhere—and not only feel self-confident but eradicate neediness from your vocabulary as well as from your being.

3. The Habit of Comparitis

Comparitis is what I call the habit of comparing ourselves to someone we think has a better life than we do. By the way, the suffix *–itis* comes from a Greek word meaning *inflammation*, and isn't it interesting that when we compare ourselves to others, we are indeed *inflaming* the emotions of jealousy and envy?

The typical thoughts of comparitis go like this: "This person is more successful/popular/better-looking/thinner/richer/more famous than me. Boy, I wish I were them."

There are three big problems with comparitis. First, you are always going to lose. It's a foregone conclusion that you're going to come up on the short end of the stick, because you are comparing yourself to someone who you think has more of something than you. Second, when you compare yourself to others, you are coming from a place of not enough. You buy into the belief that there is only so much to go around, and if someone

THIS IS WHY YOU NEED TO STOP COMPARING YOURSELF TO OTHERS.

appears to have more than you do, that means there's less for you. With scarcity thinking, you can always find evidence to back up your belief that there's not enough to go around.

Third, comparing yourself to others makes you feel bad about yourself. We are never going to look at someone who we think has more than we do and feel good about ourselves. Instead it will have the immediate and predictable effect of emotionally sapping your energy, so you end up telling yourself, "Why bother? So-and-so is better/more than me, so why even try?"

It's perfectly normal to compare ourselves to others. But just because it's normal doesn't mean it's something we should keep doing. Follow these steps and stop comparing yourself to others, because, as Theodore Roosevelt said, "Comparison is the thief of joy."

4. Perceiving Failing as Failure

Every one of us has failed at different times in our lives. Whether it was not landing that big client, saying the wrong thing at the wrong time, not speaking up when we should have, trusting the wrong people, or just making a poor decision at a critical moment, we have all done things we wish we could take back.

The problem comes when we classify these experiences as *failure*. *Failure* is a word we associate with the belief that "I didn't get what I wanted" or "I set a goal and didn't reach it." With failure comes regret, and with regret comes beating ourselves up, and with beating ourselves up comes an erosion of self-confidence, which just leads to more beating ourselves up in what I call the downward death spiral.

But hold on a moment. Let's go back to the beginning. So you didn't land that big client. Why? Did you not prepare properly? Did you try to fudge your numbers? Did you purposely mislead, or did you simply not present your case in the most convincing way?

THIS IS HOW TO LEARN FROM YOUR FAILURES.

History is filled with stories of people who "failed": they didn't get what they wanted on the first, second, third, tenth, or fiftieth try.

But they studied what caused their initial failure and then succeeded beyond their wildest dreams.

Bill Gates' first company was a total flop. Steven Spielberg applied to USC film school and was rejected twice. Jim Carrey was living in a van before he got his big break. Stephen King's first novel was rejected thirty times before he got his first acceptance letter. Michael J. Fox was selling the sections of his couch to have enough food to eat. Dwayne Johnson was down to his last seven bucks after failing to reach the NFL. The stories go on and on.

In my works, I often share stories from my own life when I fell short of my goals as examples of how to learn from my failings. As the saying goes: "There's no shame in failing. The only real failure is not trying."

5. Not Having the Right Support System

It's crucial to have the right support system in your life, career, and business. If you don't, it will be extremely difficult to build the unstoppable self-confidence that will enable you to persist through life's challenges.

I've mentioned that the more successful you become, the more people are going to come out of the woodwork and start criticizing you.

Furthermore, no matter how rich and famous and successful you get, criticism—even when it's unfounded or based on untruths—is still going to hurt.

That's why today it's more important than ever to create the right support system in your personal and professional life.

Of course, the big problem is that many people don't have this support. A 2006 study done by the University of Arizona and Duke University asked Americans how many close confidants they had. In 1985, when the first study of this kind was done, the average American reported having three close friends. In the 2004 follow-up study, the average person said they had *none*.

THIS IS WHY IT'S SO IMPORTANT TO HAVE THE RIGHT SUPPORT SYSTEM.

It's crucial to get the right support system in place to support you in the tough times and cheer you on in the good times. First, connect with like-minded individuals who share your values and aspirations, fostering relationships through networking events and online platforms. Second, seek mentors or advisors who can offer guidance and valuable insights based on their experiences. Regularly engage with them and be open to their feedback. Also, invest in professional development opportunities such as coaching, workshops, seminars, and certifications. By implementing these tips, you can cultivate a supportive network, gain valuable guidance, and continuously expand your knowledge and capabilities on your path to success.

6. The Feeling of Overwhelm

In 1968, Andy Warhol said that "In the future, everyone will be world-famous for fifteen minutes." This is where the phrase "fifteen minutes of fame" originated. That future has already arrived. Because of the ubiquity of the Internet and the advent of social media, anyone with a smartphone and Internet connection can become famous. Yet here's the problem: now that everyone can be famous, no one is. Why?

Simple math. When the people who are now considered legends of the entertainment industry were celebrities in the seventies and eighties, there were just a few television channels and no Internet.

Everyone in the United States had access to only these few choices. For example, the finale of *M*A*S*H*, on February 28, 1983, was viewed by more than 60 percent of all U.S. households. This was known as a 60 share.

Today, it is mathematically impossible for any TV show, even the Super Bowl, to get 60 share. Why? Because there are simply too many channels and too many choices for such numbers to ever be reached again.

Every day, we must make choices about how we spend our time and what we focus on, because there are an infinite number of choices and distractions available to us at the click of a mouse or tap on a smartphone.

The problem is that more you allow yourself to be distracted by these infinite choices, the less you focus on reaching your goals, and the more your self-confidence will be eroded, bit by bit.

EVERY DAY, YOU MUST CHOOSE WHERE TO PUT YOUR ATTENTION.

For example, in order to write this book for you, I had to make a conscious choice to block out time when I would not be distracted. I told the people on my team that I was not to be disturbed during certain hours of the day. I also turned off my phone, shut off my email, and unplugged from the Internet so I could focus my thoughts and write without distractions. If I hadn't set aside these distractions, it would have taken me forever to write this book. In fact, I might never have completed it.

Therefore, one of the simplest things you can do to increase your self-confidence is to eliminate distractions and give yourself the benefit of periods of focus and concentration on the task at hand.

7. Not Telling the Truth about Who You Really Are

In an earlier chapter, I showed you the difference between character and personality and discussed why it's so hard to be yourself in a world that doesn't want you to be.

We've been looking at some of the not-so-great things about the Internet and the ubiquity of social media. However, one of the great benefits of the Internet is that you can find groups of like-minded people who enjoy the same interests and hobbies you have. From left-handed ice fishermen in Wisconsin to Spider-Man fans in Ohio, the Internet gives us the ability to find and connect with other like-minded people.

Although each of us is unique and special, sometimes it's hard to express yourself when you feel you're all alone. The Internet is the single greatest communication and connection tool ever created, because it allows us to connect with people we never could have met otherwise.

First, find a coach or mentor who genuinely supports and encourages your journey of self-expression. Seek someone who understands the importance of authenticity and can provide guidance on embracing your true self. Their insights and support can help you navigate challenges and provide valuable perspectives on self-discovery.

Second, practice self-reflection and self-awareness to understand your values, passions, and strengths. Take time to identify your core beliefs and what makes you unique. Finally, find platforms or outlets that align with your interests and allow you to showcase your authentic self.

TELL THE TRUTH ABOUT WHO YOU REALLY ARE.

Whether it's through art, writing, public speaking, or any other form of creative expression, use these avenues to confidently convey your genuine thoughts, emotions, and perspectives. By following these tips, you can embark on a transformative journey of self-expression, surrounded by a supportive mentor, self-awareness, and outlets for showcasing your true essence.

8. Not Taking Inspired Action in the Face of Fear

The most common form of this is the habit of *procrastination*. The word *procrastination* is derived from the Latin *cras*, meaning *tomorrow*. Did you know that when you procrastinate, what you are doing is *tomorrowizing*?

Procrastination doesn't just mean not doing things. It means that you are not doing things that you know would be good for you. Let's say you have a project due at work. You know the deadline, yet when you go into the office, rather than working on the project, you keep finding other things to keep you busy. Remember information overload? You can always find plenty of things to keep you busy, every second of every day!

It's often hard to focus on the task at hand and usually very easy to put things off. Unfortunately we do not, as a rule, do our best work under time pressure. We often make poor decisions because the fight/flight/freeze response from our reptile brain kicks in, rather than our more rational, problem-solving brain.

THIS IS YET ANOTHER REASON TO TAKE INSPIRED ACTION IN THE FACE OF FEAR.

This is yet another reason to develop the habit of *taking inspired action in the face of fear.*

Now that you've been exposed to the Power Habits of Unstoppable Self-Confidence, let me offer you a final word of encouragement and call to action.

This book, like all of my virtual or live events and coaching programs, was created to help you advance confidently in the direction of your dreams. So what should you do now that this book is nearly over?

If you really want to get the benefits promised in this book—greater self-confidence, happier relationships, and more success in your life and business—then you must do what I've shared with you throughout this book and *take action*!

After I discovered my Afformations Method and the Power Habits System more than twenty-five years ago, I realized it was my mission and responsibility to bring this teaching to the tens of millions of people around the world who desire to create a better life for themselves, their families, and the world.

That's why I am privileged to lead private workshops and coaching programs that transform people's lives quickly and permanently. That's also why I want to personally invite you to join our one-on-one or group coaching programs.

Our coaching programs will take you to an entirely new level of success, because we actually change your relationship to self-confidence and success right there on the spot. I also show you how to break through whatever is holding you back from reaching your full potential.

You will gain the tools, skills, and strategies that will give you a new perspective on how to attract the wealth, health, relationships, and lifestyle that you've always wanted.

In fact, many of our clients count joining one of our coaching programs as one of the key turning points in their lives. It's exciting, fun, and packed with real-world skills to help you become more self-confident in every sense of the word.

The Power Habits System has been proven in thousands of real-life case studies to help people live happier, healthier, more successful lives. That's why I encourage you, to take the next logical step if you want to go further and faster!

10

For Those Who Want to Go Further and Faster

Lots of people have dreams and get knocked down and don't have things go their way. Just keep getting up and getting up, and then you WILL get your breakthrough!

—TOM BRADY

Now that this book is almost over, you have three options:

1. Forget everything you just read and let this become more "shelf-help" (not recommended).

2. Try to figure all this out on your own. Granted, it will take a lot more time and you might make a lot of costly mistakes, but you can do it on your own if you wish.

3. Do it with me so we can accelerate your results up to ten times faster with far less stress and without wasted time.

You're someone who wants to break through to the next level of success, but just aren't sure how to get there. You're someone who is ready for a change, and is willing to do whatever it takes to make it happen.

I know how you feel, because I've been there myself. In fact, I spent years struggling to achieve my goals, and I know firsthand how frustrating it can be.

Yet I also know how AMAZING it feels when you finally break through and start achieving the success you've always dreamed of.

That's why I created **Inner Game Breakthrough**, a private coaching program where I will personally teach you my iconic *Power Habits® System* that has helped my clients generate over $2.8 Billion dollars since 1997.

Here's What This Is

In this exclusive six-week group coaching program, you'll discover the exact principles, strategies and methods that have helped my clients achieve massive success in their lives, careers and relationships.

In just six short weeks, I'll give you my copy-and-paste, plug-and-play, paint-by-numbers, fill-in-the-blank templates, checklists, resources, and strategies that have generated more than *$2.8 billion* in found revenues for my clients and me since 1997.

Here's What This Will Do For You

Sometimes, our biggest opposition is ourselves. Which means you might not play bigger, simply because you believe you're not worthy of it.

That's why I've been teaching Inner Game Mastery since 1997, because without Inner Game Mastery, you won't implement. And without implementation, there's no RESULTS.

There's no lack of **INFORMATION**.

Yet there's a definite lack of **IMPLEMENTATION**.

And that leads to a lack of **TRANSFORMATION**.

That's why millions of people watch YouTube videos, read all the books and go to endless seminars, yet never experience the true, life-changing transformation that happens once you master your Inner Game.

What will this do for you? You will . . .

1. Unleash the untapped power within you and experience exponential personal growth.

2. Rewire your thought patterns, propelling you towards a life of unimagined success.

3. Demolish the inner obstacles holding you back from reaching your full potential.

4. Discover the secrets of high performers and integrate them seamlessly into your life.

5. Forge your personalized success blueprint, tailored to your unique strengths and goals.

6. Experience a dramatic boost in your confidence, making you unstoppable in every pursuit.

7. Ignite a powerful internal drive that catapults you towards your goals.

8. Transform your mindset to adopt the habits that breed success effortlessly.

9. Experience a newfound sense of freedom and control over your destiny.

10. Navigate through life's turbulence with a calm, composed mind and resilient spirit.

11. Shatter the ceiling of your perceived potential, reaching heights you never thought possible.

12. Harness your untamed inner power to influence the world around you.

13. Create an unbeatable aura of positivity that permeates every room you enter.

14. Savor the exhilarating feeling of breaking free from the chains of limiting beliefs.

15. Master the art of resilience, coming out stronger from every setback.

16. Uncover the secret to eternal happiness—living a life on your own terms.

Here's What to Do Now

Go to BreakthroughwithNoah.com and schedule your complimentary Breakthrough Consultation.

What Happens Next

After you schedule your Breakthrough Consultation, someone from my team will contact you. You'll receive our famous and legendary white-glove VIP service.

I've seen millions made even from taking the wrong actions, but I've never seen anything good come from *not* taking action.

Remember, I'm going to give you . . .

- The Right PLAN (show you what to do)
- The Right TOOLS (show you how to do it)
- The Right SUPPORT (believe in you, even if you don't believe in yourself yet)

However, I can't make you take the right actions. Only YOU can do that. Remember, if you don't have these things in place, here's what's going to happen . . .

- If you don't have the right PLAN, you'll stay **STUCK**.
- If you don't have the right TOOLS, you'll be **OVERWHELMED**.
- If you don't have the right SUPPORT, you'll feel **ALONE**.
- And if you don't take the right ACTION, what will happen is . . . **NOTHING**.

Napoleon Hill said, "Those who reach decisions promptly and definitely know what they want and generally get it. The leaders in every walk of life decide quickly and firmly."

Insurance magnate W. Clement Stone said, "The greatest enemy of wealth isn't a mindset issue. It isn't wealth or resources, it isn't even upbringing or circumstances. The greatest enemy of wealth is DELAY."

Dr. Noah St. John says, "Procrastination is the assassination of your destination."

One Final Guarantee

Ben Franklin said many years ago that there are only two guarantees in life: death and taxes. With all due respect to ol' Ben, I would argue there is, in fact, a third guarantee. It is this:

If you keep doing the same thing you're doing now, I guarantee you'll keep getting the same results you're getting now.

Therefore, if you'd like to get better results in your life and your business, I encourage you take ACTION now—because time waits for no one!

"Noah St. John's coaching starts where Think and Grow Rich *and* The Secret *left off!"*
—Mike Filsaime, 8-Figure CEO of Groovefunnels

"My company went from being stuck at $4M in sales to over $20M in sales as a result of coaching with Noah!"
—Adam S., 8-Figure CEO

"My income is up 800 percent since I started coaching with Noah!"
—Steven B., Entrepreneur

"Coaching with Noah enabled me to double my business in less than twelve months after I'd been stuck at the same level for fifteen years!"
—Aubrey R., Entrepreneur

"In the first two weeks of coaching with Noah, I TRIPLED my investment!"
—Thomesa L., Entrepreneur

"As a result of coaching with Noah, I doubled my income, then doubled it AGAIN in just twelve short weeks!"
—Mike C., Entrepreneur

YOUR FREE BONUS GIFT

As a thank-you for purchasing this book, I would like to give you exclusive, insider access to the exact system my clients are using to instantly shatter their limiting beliefs that were putting a ceiling on their business revenue, once and for all, using ONE simple process that can take as little as five minutes a day.

Best of all, it works especially well even when all the other programs, seminars, methods, systems and gurus have let you down or you don't actually know what the specific problem is.

This is also the fastest and easiest way to gain special access to the lucrative system that's added more than $2.8 billion in revenue for me and my clients since 1997.

So if you

- Want a proven system to instantly shatter limiting beliefs and recapture lost revenues

- Have a business that's beyond the start-up phase and is actually making sales
- Are ready for "hockey stick growth" in your company
- Want insider access to my fill-in-the-blank templates, checklists, and resources
- Want to know how this guaranteed system can work for you

... schedule your complimentary 7-Figure Breakthrough Consultation now, because we will review your business, see how this system can work for you, offer you some advice on how to use it, and (if we know we can help you) discuss how we can help you implement it—GUARANTEED.

Book your Breakthrough Consultation now at
BreakthroughwithNoah.com

SCAN ME

Book Noah to Speak

"Noah is definitely NOT your typical motivational speaker! I took six pages of notes during his keynote presentation. SIMPLY PHENOMENAL— A MUST-HAVE RESOURCE for every organization that wants to grow!"
—Mary Kay Cosmetics

"All I heard was great feedback! Thank you, Noah, for really engaging our audience. I am recommending you as a speaker for more meetings."
—Meeting Planners International

"I highly recommend Noah St. John as a keynote speaker because he resonates on a deep emotional level with his audience. Dynamic, impactful, inspiring, motivating, and professional— in short, the PERFECT speaker!"
—City Summit & Gala

Book Noah as your keynote speaker, and you're guaranteed to make your event highly enjoyable and unforgettable.

For more than two decades, Dr. Noah St. John has consistently rated as the number one keynote speaker by meeting planners and attendees.

His unique style combines inspiring audiences with his remarkable true story, keeping them laughing with his high-energy, down-to-earth style, and empowering them with actionable strategies to take their results to the next level.

Book Noah for
your event at
BookNoah.com

Also Available from Dr. Noah St. John

BREAKTHROUGH WITH NOAH

Discover How My Clients Are Instantly
Shattering Their Limiting Beliefs That
Were Putting A Ceiling On Their Revenue,
Once And For All, Using 1 Simple Process
That Can Take Place In As Little As
5 Minutes a Day.

BreakthroughwithNoah.com

POWER HABITS ACADEMY

Take out your head trash about money,
admit what you truly desire, and
experience your quantum leap.

PowerHabitsAcademy.com

THE AFFORMATIONS ADVANTAGE
Immediately attract more abundance on autopilot.
Afformations.com

Shop our complete line of business
and personal growth programs:
ShopNoahStJohn.com

Book Noah to speak at your virtual
or live event:
BookNoah.com

Motivate and inspire others!

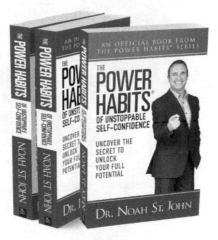

SHARE THIS BOOK!

$19.95 retail

Special quantity discounts available

To place an order, contact:

(330) 871-4331

support@SuccessClinic.com

Acknowledgments

My most grateful thanks to . . .

God, the answer to all of our questions.

My beautiful wife, Babette, for being my best friend and the best Loving Mirror I've ever had. Thank you for believing in me and supporting me and for your tireless commitment to helping me put a dent in the universe.

My parents, who sacrificed and gave more than they had.

Jack Canfield, for grokking my message when it was a bunch of pages bound with a piece of tape.

Dr. Stephen R. Covey, who inspired me to get into the business of helping people when the audiocassette album of *The 7 Habits of Highly Effective People* fell off a church bookshelf and landed at my feet. (I swear I'm not making that up.)

Through the years, many have shared ideas, inspiration, mentoring, and support that have impacted my life, each in a different way. While it's impossible to thank everyone, please know that I appreciate you greatly:

Alex Mandossian, Arianna Huffington, Donny Osmond, Gary Vaynerchuk, Jenny McCarthy, Joel Osteen, John Lee Dumas, Marie Forleo, Suze Orman, Anik Singal, Ashley Grayson, Bill and Steve Harrison, Dan Bova, Doug Crowe, Dr. Fabrizio Mancini, Harvey Mackay, Jason Hewlett, Jay Abraham, Jeff Lerner, Jeff Magee, Jen Groover, Joe Vitale, John Assaraf, John Cito, Dr. John Gray, Jon Benson, Mike Filsaime, Nathan Osmond, Neale Donald Walsch, Peter Hoppenfeld, Rich Schefren, Richard Rossi, Russell Brunson, Tom Junod, Verne Harnish, and so many other people who have inspired me in my career!

Very special thanks to the vast and growing tribe of our phenomenal coaching clients around the world who believe in the power of this message. Thank you for spreading the word about my work to all corners of the globe!

Every day, as I hear more and more stories of how the coaching work we do together is changing lives, you inspire, encourage, and uplift me.

I am humbled by your stories of how my work has changed your lives—more than you know. Whether you are a member of our coaching family, attend one of our virtual events or online trainings this year, or simply commit to telling your friends about this book, I'm grateful for you.

Every day brings with it the opportunity to be reborn in the next greatest version of ourselves.

NOW IT'S YOUR TURN

I LOOK FORWARD TO BEING A PART OF YOUR SUCCESS STORY!

About the Author

NOAH ST. JOHN, PhD is recognized as "the Father of AFFORMATIONS" and "the Mental Health Coach to the Stars."

Working with Hollywood celebrities, seven- and eight-figure CEOs, professional athletes, top executives, and elite entrepreneurs, Noah is famous for helping his coaching clients make more in 12 weeks than they did in the previous 12 months, while gaining 1–3 hours per day and 4–8 weeks a year.

Noah's clients are the 0.1 percent rock stars who love to *take action* and get amazing *results!*

Noah is also the only author in history to have works published by HarperCollins, Hay House, Simon & Schuster, Mindvalley, Nightingale-Conant, and the publisher of the *Chicken Soup for the Soul* series. His twenty-four books have been published in nineteen languages worldwide.

Noah's mission is to eliminate not-enoughness from the world. He is internationally known for his signature coaching services and facilitating workshops at companies and institutions across the globe. Noah delivers private workshops, virtual events, and online courses that his audiences call "MANDATORY for anyone who wants to succeed in life and business."

One of the most requested, in-demand business and motivational keynote speakers in the world, Noah is famous for having the Midas touch, because his clients have added more than $2.8 billion in found revenues. His sought-after advice is known as the "secret sauce" to business and personal growth.

He also appears frequently in the news worldwide, including ABC, NBC, CBS, FOX, The Hallmark Channel, National Public Radio, *Chicago Sun-Times*, *Parade*, *Los Angeles Business Journal*, *The Washington Post*, *Woman's Day*, *Entrepreneurs on Fire*, *Selling Power*, Entrepreneur.com, *The Jenny McCarthy Show*, *Costco Connection*, and *SUCCESS* magazine.

Fun fact: Noah once won an all-expenses-paid trip to Hawaii on the game show *Concentration*, where he missed winning a new car by three seconds. (Note: He had not yet discovered his AFFORMATIONS Method or Power Habits Formula.)

Book Noah to speak for your next virtual or live event, conference or seminar at **BookNoah.com**.

Printed in the USA
CPSIA information can be obtained
at www.ICGtesting.com
JSHW011918220923
49004JS00004B/20